VOLUNTARY CORPORATE LIQUIDATIONS

Recent Titles from Quorum Books

Legal Structure of International Textile Trade
Henry R. Zheng

Accounting for Data Processing Costs
Robert W. McGee

The Management of Corporate Business Units: Portfolio Strategies for Turbulent Times
Louis E. V. Nevaer and Steven A. Deck

How to Write for the Professional Journals: A Guide for Technically Trained Managers
Ryle L. Miller, Jr.

Effective Information Centers: Guidelines for MIS and IC Managers
Robert J. Thierauf

Education Incorporated: School–Business Cooperation for Economic Growth
Northeast-Midwest Institute, editor

Decision Support Systems in Finance and Accounting
H. G. Heymann and Robert Bloom

Freedom of Speech on Private Property
Warren Freedman

Causes of Failure in Performance Appraisal and Supervision: A Guide to Analysis and Evaluation for Human Resources Professionals
Joe Baker, Jr.

The Modern Economics of Housing: A Guide to Theory and Policy for Finance and Real Estate Professionals
Randall Johnston Pozdena

Productivity and Quality Through Science and Technology
Y. K. Shetty and Vernon M. Buehler, editors

Interactive Corporate Compliance: An Alternative to Regulatory Compulsion
Jay A. Sigler and Joseph Murphy

VOLUNTARY CORPORATE LIQUIDATIONS

Ronald J. Kudla

Q

QUORUM BOOKS

New York · Westport, Connecticut · London

Library of Congress Cataloging-in-Publication Data

Kudla, Ronald J.
  Voluntary corporate liquidations / Ronald J. Kudla.
    p.   cm.
  Includes index.
  ISBN 0-89930-275-0 (lib. bdg. : alk. paper)
  1. Liquidation—United States. I. Title.
KF1475.K83   1988
346.73′0662—dc19   87-32282
[347.306662]

British Library Cataloguing in Publication Data is available.

Library of Congress Catalog Card Number: 87-32282
ISBN: 0-89930-275-0

First published in 1988 by Quorum Books

Greenwood Press, Inc.
88 Post Road West, Westport, Connecticut 06881

Printed in the United States of America

The paper used in this book complies with the
Permanent Paper Standard issued by the National
Information Standards Organization (Z39.48-1984).

10 9 8 7 6 5 4 3 2 1

Copyright Acknowledgments

The publisher and author are grateful to the following for granting use of their material:

Table 4.1, reprinted from Stanley Hagendorf, *Tax Manual for Corporate Liquidations, Redemptions, and Estate Planning Recapitalizations,* Prentice-Hall, Inc., 1978, Englewood Cliffs, New Jersey, pp. 91–92, is courtesy of Garland Publishing, Inc., New York, and Stanley Hagendorf.

Table 5.1, reprinted from "The Effect of Voluntary Corporate Liquidation on Shareholder Wealth," by Terrance R. Skantz and Roberto Marchesini, *Journal of Financial Research* 10, no. 1 (Spring 1987): 74, is courtesy of the publisher.

Extracts from chapter 6 are taken from "A Company That's Worth More Dead Than Alive," Peter W. Bernstein, *Fortune,* February 26, 1979, pp. 43–44. Reprinted courtesy of *Fortune.*

Financial assistance for purchasing the liquidating proxies cited in chapter 1 was provided by the University of Wisconsin–Eau Claire Faculty Development and Curriculum Improvement Grant Program.

To my wife, Mary
and
my children, Hilary, Allison, and Thomas

Contents

Tables

VOLUNTARY CORPORATE LIQUIDATIONS

1

Introduction

A voluntary corporate liquidation involves selling all of the firm's asssets for cash, paying all outstanding debts from the proceeds, and distributing the remaining funds to stockholders as liquidating dividends. The corporate entity of the liquidating firm ceases to exist after liquidation. This type of divestiture is in contrast to sell-offs, where the selling firm remains as a going concern and retains its corporate identity.

Although voluntary corporate liquidations are rare, a growing number of firms have liquidated in recent years, including Kaiser Industries Corporation, UV Industries, Inc., Reeves Telecom, Bates Manufacturing Company, Inc., and Telecor. A partial list of voluntary corporate liquidations is shown in Table 1.1. Much of the data for this book is based on a careful analysis of liquidating proxies for many of these firms.

The purpose of this book is to provide information to corporate executives that may be useful in evaluating the suitability of liquidation as a strategic planning tool. In addition, the book is useful as a reference for executives actually involved in liquidations. A comprehensive literature search disclosed very limited published information on voluntary corporate liquidations.

A wave of corporate restructuring has occurred in the United States in recent years. This restructuring has taken many forms including acquisitions, mergers, spin-offs, sell-offs, cutbacks, leveraged buy-outs, and friendly and hostile takeovers. The goal of the restructuring is to make American corporations more productive

Table 1.1

A Partial List of Voluntary Corporate Liquidations, 1963–1982

Liquidating Firm	Liquidation Announcement Date
American Recreation Group, Inc.	Aug. 19, 1975
Aguirre Company	Mar. 9, 1977
Ambassador Oil	Jan. 12, 1965
American Manufacturing	Sept. 19, 1979
Apco Oil	Nov. 13, 1975
Austral Oil	Mar. 22, 1977
Automatic Service Company	May 11, 1976
Barber Oil Company	Oct. 3, 1980
Bates Manufacturing	Jan. 18, 1979
Barton Brands, Inc.	Jun. 1, 1971
Bayuk Cigars	Jun. 22, 1981
Bayview Oil	April 1, 1964
Bridge Street Inc.	Sept. 19, 1973
Bristol Brass Corporation	Jun. 13, 1979
California Financial Corporation	Jan. 19, 1976
Canadian International Power	Dec. 12, 1976
CHC Corporation	Feb. 10, 1977
Chemical Enterprise	July 19, 1966
Congoleum Corporation	Dec. 20, 1979
Consolidated Coal Inc.	Oct. 13, 1965
Cott Corporation	Sept. 27, 1978
DCL Inc.	Feb. 21, 1979
DeJur Amsco	Dec. 31, 1976
Deltec International Ltd.	Dec. 31, 1976
Detroit Gasket & Manufacturing	Jan. 13, 1977
Drilling & Exploration Company	Dec. 3, 1964
Edgington Oil	June 1, 1976
Empire Financial	Mar. 12, 1974
Fuller, G.A. Company	April 7, 1965
Furman Wolfson Corporation	Sept. 12, 1968

Table 1.1 (continued)

Great Basins Petroleum	Jun. 7, 1979
Great Western Producers Inc.	Dec. 30, 1964
Griesedieck	May 8, 1975
Hanna M.A. Company	Oct. 8, 1965
Harucel Inc.	Jan. 17, 1973
Holyoke Shares Inc.	May 12, 1967
House of Ronnie, Inc.	Mar. 13, 1981
International Oil & Gas Company	Sept. 30, 1965
Kaiser Industries	May 6, 1976
Kenilworth Realty	May 16, 1980
Keystone Industries	Jun. 2, 1977
Kirby Industries	Nov. 19, 1974
Klion (H.L.) Inc.	April 14, 1965
Manning, Maxwell & Moore	Aug. 18, 1964
Merritt Chapman & Scott	Mar. 22, 1966
McKeon Construction	Sept. 26, 1980
National Liberty Corporation	Jun. 12, 1980
National Silver	Jan. 17, 1980
OKC Corporation	July 12, 1979
Paco Inc.	Oct. 8, 1963
Pasco Inc.	May 22, 1975
Patagonia Corporation	July 22, 1980
Republic Aviation	April 1, 1965
Reeves Telecom	Jan. 19, 1979
RH Medical Services	Aug. 28, 1980
Rockower Brothers, Inc.	Mar. 10, 1978
Rossmoor Corporation	Jan. 25, 1980
Rowlands Products, Inc.	Jan. 13, 1975
Reliance Manufacturing Company	Jun. 16, 1964
St. Johnsbury Trucking	Oct. 14, 1974
Shenandoah Oil Corporation	April 5, 1978
Steel Parts Corporation	Sept. 8, 1964
Sterling Brewers Inc.	May 5, 1964

Table 1.1 (continued)

Telecor Inc.	Mar. 10, 1978
Texas Gulf Producing	Sept. 3, 1963
Texas Pacific Coal & Oil	Feb. 12, 1963
Tishman Realty & Construction	Oct. 1, 1976
Trav-Ler Industries	Jun. 9, 1964
U.V. Industries	Jan. 19, 1979
United States Realty Investments	Feb. 18, 1981
Universal Marion	July 10, 1968
Vita Foods	July 10, 1968
Wakefield Corporation	Aug. 31, 1965
Westates Petroleum	Mar. 7, 1975
Yonkers Raceway	Mar. 24, 1972

Source: Professor John Schatzberg, University of Arizona, Tucson, Arizona

and competitive. Voluntary corporate liquidation can be viewed as another type of corporate restructuring that should not be ignored by corporate executives. Liquidation was the preferred strategic alternative for the companies examined in this book.

Corporate liquidations can be voluntary or involuntary. Involuntary liquidations occur when a company is bankrupt or unable to meet its fixed contractual debt obligations.[1] As an example, when a company fails to make interest payments or sinking fund payments on outstanding bonds, the company is in default and can be forced into bankruptcy by the bondholders. Firms that voluntarily liquidate, however, are oftentimes financially healthy. This book is only concerned with voluntary corporate liquidations.

Managements would not undertake voluntary liquidations unless they expected them to increase shareholder wealth. In other words, the companies are worth more dead than alive. By selling off the assets of the company piecemeal, the liquidation proceeds that are distributed to shareholders typically exceed the market value of their common stock shares. Accordingly, all stockholders benefit from the liquidation. Chapter 2 explains in detail the motives for voluntary corporate liquidations.

An example of a voluntary corporate liquidation is Overseas National Airways, Inc. (ONA).[2] ONA operated commercial passenger and cargo charter flights in the United States and foreign countries for thirty years. The principal assets of the company were three DC-10 aircraft and related equipment. The company's net operating revenue in 1977 was approximately $80 million.

The decision by ONA's board of directors to liquidate the firm was due to several factors. One of the major factors was the introduction by U.S. and foreign scheduled carriers of government-approved, deeply discounted fares in the company's principal foreign and domestic markets. The flood of low fares seriously eroded the market for the company's charters and contributed to the company's disappointing financial results. Operating losses of $27 million were incurred by the firm in the five years and six months ended June 26, 1978, including $3.5 million during the first six months of 1978. In addition, ONA was faced with sharply rising operating costs and above-average insurance rates.

Another factor that influenced the liquidation decision was the current market value of the company's DC-10 aircraft, which was substantially in excess of the company's book value for these assets, and the uncertainties in predicting the market value of DC-10 aircraft in the future. The demand for these aircraft significantly increased as scheduled airline companies searched for available planes to satisfy demand for low ticket prices. The price for used jets available for immediate delivery had risen rapidly because of inflation and long waits for delivery of new planes. Because the sale of the company's DC-10 aircraft would result in the company's having no operating assets and its principal assets would be cash and securities, the board concluded that liquidation was in the best interests of the company's stockholders. The liquidation proceeds were estimated to be more than double the market value of the company's common stock.

As was true for other liquidations discussed in this book, approval of the plan of liquidation and dissolution by ONA's board of directors was facilitated by corporate insiders who owned a significant amount of the company's outstanding common stock. In the case of ONA, principal stockholders, officers, and directors owned 49 percent of the outstanding stock. All stockholders benefited from the liquidation because the liquidation value exceeded the market value of the firm, but insiders realized a larger dollar increase in wealth because they owned a larger fraction of the firm's outstanding shares.

The remainder of this book is devoted to a detailed examination of various aspects of voluntary corporate liquidations. Chapter 2 describes and illustrates with multiple examples motives that corporate executives have given for undertaking liquidations. Chapter 3 covers various mechanical aspects of liquidations including the plan of liquidation and dissolution, the proxy statement, and the liquidating trust agreement. Employment arrangements for the liquidating firm's employees, treatment of unexercised stock options, and the hiring of experts are also discussed. Chapter 4 reviews the tax aspects of liquidations while Chapter 5 examines whether liquidations have resulted in increases in shareholder wealth.

Chapter 6 provides three case studies of individual liquidations. In each of these liquidations, management was frustrated with depressed stock prices, which it believed understated the company's true or intrinsic value. The liquidation of Kaiser Industries Corporation was undertaken to give greater security value to the stockholders. The company's relatively low stock price was due primarily to the poor performance of Kaiser Steel, a company in which Kaiser Industries had a controlling interest. UV Industries, Inc., was liquidated to achieve major tax savings and to avoid a potential hostile takeover. The liquidation of Tishman Realty and Construction Company, Inc., was completed to avoid accounting rules that caused the security markets to undervalue its real estate properties. Chapter 7 provides a summary of the book that highlights the major findings and conclusions.

NOTES

1. "Biggest Liquidator of Them All," *Forbes*, February 15, 1977, pp. 55–56.

2. "Overseas National Exits in Style," *Business Week*, October 2, 1978, p. 36.

2

The Decision to Liquidate

The principal reason given by corporate executives for the liquidation decision is that the liquidation proceeds to be distributed to common stockholders exceed the market value of their shares. This chapter explains the disparity in liquidation values and market values and describes the causative factors underlying corporate liquidation decisions. These factors include: (1) tax factors, (2) regulatory factors, (3) market factors, (4) competition, (5) cessation of business, and (6) government intervention. Of course various combinations of these factors were operative in most corporate liquidations, but the intent is to classify liquidations by the perceived degree of importance of these factors.

Although the circumstances surrounding corporate liquidations are highly varied, most liquidations had three common characteristics. First, there was favorable tax treatment under Section 337 of the Internal Revenue Code of 1954 on gains from the sale of corporate assets. Second, there was a willing buyer for the liquidating firm or its assets. The assets of the liquidating firm were typically sold piecemeal. Oftentimes the buyer was willing to pay a premium for the liquidating firm because the firm was worth more to the buyer than to the seller. Third, the liquidation decision was greatly facilitated by significant insider ownership of common stock in the liquidating firm. Insiders included officers, directors, and owners of significant amounts of the common stock of companies.

By identifying the factors that contributed to corporate liquidations and describing various liquidation scenarios, corporate executives will be in a better position to evaluate the merits and risks of liquidation as a strategic alternative for their companies. The voluntary corporate liquidation decisions described in this chapter were rational, well-planned and in the best interests of the common stockholders. Much of the information contained in this chapter was gleaned from an analysis of liquidating proxies and other published information.

TAX FACTORS

A major stimulus to voluntary corporate liquidations was favorable tax treatment of gains on the sale of corporate assets. According to Section 337 of the Internal Revenue Code of 1954, any gain or loss on the sale or exchange of a company's assets is nontaxable to the company provided that the company adopts a plan of complete liquidation and dissolution prior to the sale of its assets, and that thereafter all of the company's assets, except assets retained to meet claims against the company, are fully distributed to shareholders within one year after adoption of the plan.

The amounts distributed to shareholders in complete liquidation are treated as in full payment in exchange for their stock. Distributions received by stockholders are treated as a capital transaction and a capital gain or loss is reportable for Federal income tax purposes.

The tax advantage to the corporation was one of the most frequently cited reasons for the liquidation decision in the liquidating proxies that were examined. However, the Tax Reform Act of 1986 effectively eliminates this advantage by requiring that the sale of the liquidating firm's assets be viewed as a taxable transaction to the firm. The likely effects of this change in tax laws will be to discourage future liquidations motivated mainly by tax factors, require the liquidating firm to receive a higher premium for its assets, or make other motives for liquidation more important.

REGULATORY FACTORS

Deregulation influenced several corporate liquidations. The effect of the deregulation was to make it more difficult for some smaller firms to effectively compete with larger firms which had much greater financial resources.

An example of liquidation in the motor carrier industry was Merchants, Inc., which owned a system of common carriers engaged in motor carrier operations. The system engaged in the transportation of general commodities, petroleum and petroleum-based products, gypsum products, and related building materials. Merchants' board of directors decided to sell the company's assets to the Meridian Companies for approximately $58.5 million in cash and then to liquidate the company. Among the factors that the board considered in arriving at its decision was the uncertain environment in which the motor carrier industry operated. This environment was created by the introduction of proposed federal legislation aimed at partial or complete deregulation of the motor carrier industry and uncertainty over the future availability and cost of gasoline and diesel fuel. Other factors that the board considered included the opportunity for all shareholders to receive cash for their investment upon liquidation following the sale of the assets and the opportunity for large stockholders to diversify their investments. Since the purchase price of the company's assets exceeded the market value of the company's common stock and the transaction was to be nontaxable to the company, the board concluded that the liquidation was desirable.

Tishman Realty and Construction Company, Inc., was one of the largest publicly held real estate companies engaged in the ownership and operation of commercial properties. One of the main reasons that Tishman's board of directors sold most of its properties and liquidated the company was that the company's common stock traded in public securities markets at a price that did not reflect the underlying value of the assets of the corporation. Tishman's management believed that this undervaluation was due to accounting rules that forced many publicly held real estate companies to carry their properties, mostly large office buildings, on the books at historic cost minus depreciation, when most of these properties had appreciated substantially and generated a large cash flow. The result was that investors did not have the necessary information to properly value the company's common stock.

The remaining assets that Tishman did not sell were transferred to a newly organized limited partnership. The partnership provided several advantages including: (1) the ability of the partnership to make distributions to its partners from cash flow that is expected to be greater than the ability of the corporation to pay dividends to its shareholders, (2) the partnership will not be subject to income tax, (3) the partnership distributions will receive more favorable tax treatment than do corporate dividends, and (4) the partners would be free of requirements for public disclosure.

The liquidation of Bates Manufacturing Company, Inc., a company engaged in the leasing and contracting of owned coal lands in Virginia and Kentucky, was precipitated by new strip mining laws, which caused a shift from strip mining to deep mining of the firm's coal reserves. This shift would substantially increase the firm's capital expenditures. Accordingly, the board of directors of Bates believed that it was expedient for the firm to sell its assets and liquidate.

MARKET FACTORS

Several firms liquidated because of unfavorable market conditions that adversely affected their current operations and future outlook. An example was Rossmoor Corporation, a real estate developer specializing in the development of planned residential communities for sale and related commercial projects for lease. At the time of Rossmoor's liquidation decision, the company had a substantial amount of cash available from the sale of several real estate projects. The company's board of directors was faced with a choice between planning for the investment of the cash proceeds in new residential or commercial real estate development or liquidating the company and distributing the proceeds from the sale of the company's assets to its shareholders. The board of directors opted for the liquidation alternative because of the unfavorable economic outlook for real estate development.

In evaluating the real estate investment alternative, Rossmoor's board of directors considered a number of factors including the scarcity of real estate that could be profitably developed, recent dramatic increases in the cost of construction and construction and mortgage financing, and the relatively low market value of the company's common stock compared with the estimated per-share liquidation value after sale of the company's assets. The cost of real estate development had also increased because of required compliance with numerous laws, ordinances, and regulations relating to approvals and land use entitlements. The combined effect of federal, state, and local laws was to make the real estate development process complex, uncertain, and expensive.

Another development that made real estate investment less attractive was the dramatic increase in the cost of mortgage financing to consumers. Many mortgage companies were unwilling to make fixed-rate, long-term mortgages because of exceptionally high and volatile interest rates. The high interest rates priced many potential buyers out of the market while alternative mortgage financing techniques such as variable interest rates and graduated payments were far less attractive to prospective buyers.

COMPETITION

A high incidence of corporate liquidations occurred in the oil and gas industry during the 1970s and early 1980s because of increased competition in this industry. Among the oil and gas companies that liquidated during this period were Apco Oil Corporation, Austral Oil Company, Barber Oil Corporation, Great Basins Petroleum Company, Kirby Industries, Inc., Pasco, Inc., Shenandoah Oil Corporation, and Westates Petroleum Company. Most of these firms were independent oil and gas companies that were faced with intense competition from much larger firms with far greater resources. The smaller firms could not raise the large amounts of capital required for oil and gas exploration and development.

The future of the smaller firms was also adversely affected by the proliferation of restrictive government regulations and controls including regulation by the Federal Energy Administration and Federal Power Commission. One of these regulations controlled the price of natural gas sold to interstate pipeline companies. Proposed changes in tax laws such as repeal of the depletion allowance were also detrimental to the smaller firms. These developments significantly reduced the operational flexibility, profitability, and attractiveness to investors of independent oil and gas companies.

Although the risk of doing business was greater because of regulatory and tax factors and competition was keen, the value of oil and gas reserves and refining properties held by the smaller companies increased substantially. In most cases the buyers of these properties were large integrated oil companies that had their own petroleum production, refining, and marketing facilities. These properties were worth more to the larger companies because they had the vast financial resources necessary to engage in oil and gas exploration and development. The liquidation decisions were made because the value that might be obtained for the shareholders through the sale of the firm's assets and distribution to the shareholders of the proceeds likely would exceed the market value of their stock based on past trading of such stock when there was no merger or liquidation activity.

Increased competition in other industries also resulted in corporate liquidations. The board of directors of Rowland, Inc., approved the sale of its polycarbonate assets to the Rohm and Haas Company and liquidated the company because the alternative of continuing in business exposed the company to the risk of adverse long-term consequences that might result from increased competition and increased capital investment needs. The board concluded that future capital requirements of the polycarbonate sheet operations and ownership of raw material sources by the company's major competitor would place smaller companies such as Rowland with limited capital resources at a competitive disadvantage. Because the firm's financial condition at the time of the liquidation decision was at a historic high and there was no assurance that business would continue at existing high levels, the board believed that it was an opportune time to sell the company's assets and liquidate the company.

CESSATION OF BUSINESS

Cessation of business was the primary reason for the liquidation of Rockower Brothers, Inc., and Telecor, Inc. The principal assets of Rockower were men's and boys' clothing departments operated in 147 of Woolworth's Woolco discount department stores. Rockower operated these stores under license agreements with the F. W. Woolworth Company. When Woolworth announced its intention to cancel and terminate the license agreements for these stores, Rockower agreed to sell substantially all of its operating assets to Woolworth and liquidate the company. Rockower's board of directors considered various alternatives to liquidation, principally involving the acquisition of or merger with other businesses, but did not find any alternative preferable to liquidation, especially considering the favorable tax consequences as provided under Section 337 of the Internal Revenue Code of 1954. Accordingly, the liquidation plan was deemed to be in the best interests of the shareholders.

Telecor's Newcraft, Inc., subsidiary was the exclusive distributor of certain Panasonic products in the western United States. This distributionship business represented approximately 88 percent of Telecor's total revenues. The distribution agreements were made with the Panasonic Corporation, a wholly owned subsidiary of the Panasonic Company Division of Matsushita Electric Corporation of America (MECA). When MECA announced its intention not to renew the distribution agreements with Newcraft, Telecor's management elected to sell its assets to Panasonic and liquidate the company. Telecor's liquidating proxy did not contain any discussion of alternatives to liquidation. Given Telecor's heavy reliance on the Panasonic product line, MECA's actions effectively terminated Telecor's business and therefore liquidation was viewed as advantageous.

GOVERNMENT INTERVENTION

The liquidation of the Aguirre Company was a consequence of expropriation of the company's principal assets by the government of Puerto Rico. Aguirre had been engaged in the production of raw and semi-refined sugar, blackstrap molasses, certain vegetables, and related operations in Puerto Rico, but the government of Puerto Rico expropriated the sugar and sugar-related assets of the company, including 13,000 acres of land. Expropriation compensation amounted to approximately $36.5 million. Following the expropriation, the principal activities of Aguirre were agricultural and industrial equipment sales and the importation and distribution of construction materials at wholesale and retail levels.

Aguirre's board of directors had explored other alternatives to liquidation but found them to be less beneficial to the interests of the company's shareholders. These alternatives included increasing existing business activities and merger with, acquisition of, or acquisition by other companies. In this connection, investment banking firms were contacted and approaches were made directly to certain public companies that might have an interest. Preliminary exploratory discussions with more than thirty companies and interested parties did not result in any viable offers.

Other factors that were considered in the liquidation decision included the current economic conditions in Puerto Rico, lack of willing purchasers for the company's remaining businesses on acceptable terms, inability to develop profitable new lines of business, unfavorable tax consequences of partial liquidation, and the desire expressed by numerous shareholders to receive a cash return on their investment.

OTHER FACTORS

Other factors that contributed to complete corporate liquidations included the failure of companies to achieve adequate profitability (e.g., Dejur-Amsco Corporation and Cott Corporation), management's desire to give shareholders a direct ownership interest in shares held by a holding company (Cowles Communications, Inc.) and loss of control considerations (American Manufacturing Company, Inc.).

Dejur-Amsco Corporation engaged in importing and distributing a varied line of dictating and transcribing machines and accessories under exclusive distributorship arrangements. This equipment was sold through 350 business equipment products dealers in the United States. The company's board of directors decided to liquidate the company primarily because of the company's failure to obtain consistent profitability and earn a satisfactory return on invested capital. The board was also influenced by the limited and illiquid market for the company's shares, the relatively high cost of continuing as a public company, and the competitive disadvantages due to its narrow product line. When the company received an offer to purchase its assets for a price significantly greater than the trading value of its shares, the board recommended the sale and subsequent liquidation of the company. The purchaser of the assets was a larger company engaged in the same line of business.

Another liquidation that was caused by unacceptable profitability was the Cott Corporation, which was owned by Fuqua Industries, Inc., a diversified manufacturing, distribution, and service company. Cott Corporation was engaged in the production and distribution of carbonated beverages under the "Cott" brand and its other trademarks and under private label brands. The liquidation was facilitated by Fuqua's 83.7 percent controlling interest in Cott's shares. In making the liquidation decision, Fuqua determined that Cott's business and prospects were not consistent with Fuqua's corporate and financial objectives. Not only did Cott have low historic profitability but it was a regional bottler that faced intense competition from national beverage companies. Accordingly, Fuqua's board concluded that the liquidation was in the best interests of all of Cott's stockholders.

The principal investment of Cowles Communications, Inc., consisted of a block of 2,600,000 shares of common stock in the New York Times Company (hereafter referred to as the Times). The company's operations comprised two television stations owned and operated by a wholly owned subsidiary, Cowles Broadcasting, Inc. (CBI). Cowles' board of directors decided that direct ownership by the company's shareholders of the Times stock and CBI stock would better serve their interests than their indirect ownership through the present investment company structure which served no independent economic purpose. The board concluded that liquidation was the preferred method of accomplishing direct ownership particularly in light of the tax consequences when compared with the tax consequences of other possibilities for achieving direct ownership.

Among the assets held by the American Manufacturing Company, Inc. (AMCI), was 3,215,748 common stocks in Eltra Corporation, which represented 28 percent of Eltra's outstanding shares. This ownership gave AMCI effective control of Eltra. Eltra was a diversified manufacturer of electrical, consumer, and industrial goods. AMCI's board of directors decided to sell the Eltra shares to AC Holding Corporation, a wholly owned subsidiary of Allied Chemical Corporation, because it appeared that if a tender offer was made directly to stockholders of Eltra, the maker of such an offer could acquire more than 51 percent of the outstanding common stock of Eltra, which would put AMCI in the position of owning a minority interest in Eltra with the associated risks of such a minority position. AMCI's board determined that it was advisable to sell the shares and liquidate the company in light of the favorable tax consequences associated with complete liquidation and in consideration of the favorable relationship between the price to be paid by AC Holding for the Eltra shares and the prices at which Eltra common stock traded on the New York Stock Exchange prior to any tender offer, merger, or liquidation activity.

SUMMARY

The liquidation decision is typically a corporate response to a combination of factors that adversely affect a firm's current operations and future outlook. These factors include increased competition, regulatory effects, and market factors. Although each corporate liquidation decision has unique characteristics, most liquidations had three common characteristics. First, there was favorable tax treatment on gains from the sale of corporate assets under Section 337 of the Internal Revenue Code of 1954. However, this tax advantage has been largely eliminated by the Tax Reform Act of 1986, which requires that the gains on the sale of a liquidating firm's assets be treated as taxable to the firm. Second, there was a willing buyer for the liquidating firm or its assets. Oftentimes the buyer was willing to pay a premium to the seller because the firm was worth more to the buyer than to the seller. An example is a large integrated oil company buying a smaller independent oil company that did not have the resources necessary to engage in oil and gas exploration and development. Finally, the liquidation decision was facilitated by significant insider ownership of common stock in the liquidating firm. Insiders include officers, directors, and owners of a significant amount of a company's common stock.

Other factors that contributed to the liquidation decision include the desire to provide all shareholders with cash for their investment and to give large stockholders the opportunity to diversify their investments particularly when an illiquid market exists, cessation of business resulting from cancellation of license and lease agreements, loss of control considerations, failure to achieve adequate profitability, and government expropriation of assets.

The voluntary corporate liquidation decision is rational, well-planned, and in the best interests of the common stockholders. The factors described in this chapter will aid management in evaluating the merits and risks of the liquidation alternative. As has been shown, liquidation was the preferred strategic alternative for the companies that were examined, and in all cases the common stockholders approved the plan of liquidation and dissolution.

3

Mechanics of Corporate Liquidations

This chapter provides an overview of the process by which a voluntary liquidation is effected. The chapter is intended not to be a comprehensive guide, but rather to provide information on many of the most important technical aspects of liquidations. Executives who are contemplating a complete liquidation will find this information useful.

A key document in the liquidation process, which is discussed in this chapter, is the plan of liquidation and dissolution. Other aspects of liquidation that are covered in this chapter include the proxy statement, liquidating trust agreement, use of legal, accounting, and other experts, and employee arrangements.

NOTICE OF SPECIAL MEETING OF STOCKHOLDERS

Each shareholder is sent a notice of a special meeting of shareholders. The purposes of the meeting are to: (1) consider and vote upon a plan of complete liquidation and dissolution of the company, (2) approve an agreement to sell substantially all of the assets of the company to designated buyers, (3) authorize an amendment to the certification of incorporation of the company to change its corporate name, and (4) transact such other business as may properly come before the meeting. An example of this notice is from the House of Ronnie, Inc., shown as Appendix A.

The notice of the special meeting of shareholders indicates the date, time, and place of the meeting and states the holder of record date for stockholders who are entitled to vote at the meeting. The management and board of directors of the company usually recommend approval and adoption of the plan of complete liquidation and dissolution. Typically, a majority vote of shareholders is required to approve the plans. Stockholders who cannot attend the special meeting are urged to read the accompanying proxy statement and to complete, sign, date, and return the accompanying proxy. The corporate name change is necessary because the company is being liquidated, or the corporate name is being sold.

THE PLAN OF LIQUIDATION AND DISSOLUTION

The plan of liquidation and dissolution provides stockholders with relevant information on all aspects of the proposed liquidation. The plan is typically included with a proxy statement, which is sent to all stockholders. The plan is voted upon either at the annual meeting of the stockholders or as previously noted at a special meeting that is called by the officers of the liquidating firm.

Appendix B provides a summary of the proposed plan of liquidation and dissolution for Bates Manufacturing Company, Inc., and Appendix C shows the complete plan for the Austral Oil Company. As shown in these appendixes, the plan provides detailed information on the firm's business, its principal stockholders, how the firm will be liquidated, reasons for the liquidation, the opinions of legal experts, and selected financial data.

Historically, voluntary liquidations were structured to qualify for preferential tax treatment under Section 337 of the Internal Revenue Code, which allowed the corporation to avoid taxes on most gains. This section required the corporation to sell substantially all of its assets in the twelve-month period following shareholder adoption of the plan of complete liquidation. During that twelve-month period, the liquidating firm sets aside a reasonable fund to meet claims against the company including unascertained or contingent liabilities and expenses. The proceeds from the sale of assets are distributed pro-rata to the firm's stockholders. Any partial distributions are one of a series of two or more distributions in complete liquidation.

An important component of the plan of complete liquidation is the agreement to sell the assets of the liquidating firm to a designated buyer. An example of this agreement is shown as Appen-

By writing the Securities and Exchange Commission directly, a
heaper but less speedy type of service is available. The charge is
0.10 per page plus shipping costs with a $5 minimum charge. Ser-
ce is usually provided within two weeks but sometimes delays of
much as two additional weeks are experienced. Disclosure, Inc.,
the contractor for this service.

IPLOYMENT ARRANGEMENTS FOR THE
QUIDATING FIRM'S EMPLOYEES

mployment arrangements for the liquidating firm's employees
highly varied and depend on the particular circumstances in-
ed in each liquidation. If the buyer of the liquidating firm's
ts plans to operate the business as a going concern, the buyer
offer employment to substantially all of the firm's employees
eir current wage and salary rates. The employees are also given
ance, vacation, retirement, and other benefits equivalent to those
e company. In addition, the buyer will assume the company's
ations under all existing collective bargaining agreements. If,
ver, assets are sold for their salvage value and not operated for
, in most cases, employees lose their jobs.
en employees lose their jobs, they typically are given sever-
pay. For example, at Barber Oil Corporation, severance pay
ne week for three months of service up to twenty-four weeks
ployees having five or more years of service. At OKC Cor-
on, a bonus of up to six months of salary was given to key
yees. Apco Oil Corporation and Austral Oil Company paid
nance bonuses to employees in recognition of past services
e company. In some liquidations, compensation arrange-
re made to retain employees who are necessary to facilitate
idation process. Some officers, directors, and managers of
idating firm may continue in their present capacities with
ng firm at salary levels adjusted to reflect any additional or
duties. Examples include officers of Cowles Communica-
rcata Corporation, St. Johnsbury Trucking Company,
ts, Inc., and Kirby Industries, Inc.
lly, unexercised stock options held by employees are sold
the liquidating firm. As consideration for such sale, the
receives an amount equal to the amount by which the op-
cise price is exceeded by the market price of the firm's

dix D. Appendix D contains the agreement for the
ties by and between Austral Oil Company and T
Company. If at the end of the twelve-month peri
assets that have not been sold, these assets are tra
uidating trust which is formed by the firm's boar
the benefit of the stockholders. The purposes of th
are to: (1) collect, liquidate, or otherwise conver
ceivables, debts, claims, and assets of the compa
charge all debts, claims, obligations, liabilities, a
company, and (3) distribute to the stockholders
remaining in the hands of the trustees. To illust
trust agreement for the Barber Oil Corporation
pendix E.

OBTAINING DOCUMENTS FROM THE SE
AND EXCHANGE COMMISSION

Managers contemplating liquidation of the
ested in obtaining copies of proxy stateme
ments, or annual reports for companies t
dated. These documents are public reco
Securities and Exchange Commission. The
obtain this information is from Disclosure
Bethesda, Maryland 20816 (telephone num
951–1350; toll-free number outside Maryl
closure also has offices in New York City
(312–902–1550), and Los Angeles (213–9
Disclosure provides several types of ser
a demand deposit account by depositing
whenever the customer needs reports,
possible with the fee being automatic
count. Each month the customer recei
activity on the account. Current filir
1968 are available on paper or microfic
service for paper copies costs $0.35
order) or $10 per filing on microfic
each, and 10-Ks and registration sta
charges are extra. Air courier, mess
also available. Other on-demand s
are foreign company annual report

stock immediately preceding the declaration of the first liquidating dividend. This amount is multiplied by the number of common stock shares per option. The stock option plans are then terminated.

LEGAL, ACCOUNTING, AND OTHER EXPERTS

The directors of the liquidating firm may retain accounting, legal, and other experts and pay such experts fees and expenses to carry out the purposes and intentions of the plan. These fees and expenses may be incurred in negotiating and drafting various agreements, filings, and other documents and litigating actions brought by and against the firm. Public accountants examine the financial records of the firm. Legal counsel prepares the plan of liquidation, registration statement, application for IRS rulings, and other documents, and it reviews the tax consequences of the liquidation.

Other experts in addition to lawyers and accountants may also be employed. Investment bankers are typically retained to opine as to the fairness to the stockholders of the liquidating firm of the financial terms of proposed transactions involving the sale of the firm's assets. In some liquidations, more than one investment banker is retained, such as the use of Goldman, Sachs & Company and Oppenheimer & Company by Pasco, Inc. Examples of these opinion letters are shown in Appendix F.

4

Tax Aspects of Corporate Liquidations

This chapter covers the highlights of the tax laws that govern corporate liquidations. Because corporate liquidations are among the most complex of business transactions, the reader is advised to seek the counsel of a tax expert in connection with each liquidation.

THE TAX REFORM ACT OF 1986

Prior to the Tax Reform Act of 1986, Section 337 of the Internal Revenue Code (IRC) of 1954 stated that any gain or loss on the sale or exchange of a company's assets is nontaxable to the company provided that the company adopts a plan of complete liquidation prior to the sale of its assets and that thereafter all of the company's assets, except assets retained to meet claims against the company, are fully distributed to shareholders within one year after adoption of the plan.

The Tax Reform Act of 1986 repealed the twelve-month liquidation provisions of IRC Section 337 by requiring that gain or loss is generally recognized by a corporation upon the liquidating distribution or sale of its assets unless an exception applies.[1] A corporation recognizes gain or loss upon a distribution of property in complete liquidation as if it had sold the property to the distributee at its fair market value. If the property is distributed subject to a liability, or if the distributee assumes a liability upon the distribution, the fair market value of the property cannot be less, for purposes of determining gain or loss, than the amount of the liability.

An exception to the general rule requiring gain or loss recognition applies to controlled subsidiaries. If a corporation owns all the stock of a subsidiary that liquidates under Section 332, the subsidiary recognizes no gain or loss.[2] The reason that this liquidation is a nonrecognition event is that the controlled subsidiary is liquidated into its parent corporation and represents an intercorporate transfer. Because the parent corporation takes a carryover basis under IRC Section 334 (b) (1), all the gain will be subject to future corporate tax.

If a subsidiary liquidates under IRC Section 332 but has minority shareholders, the results for the subsidiary are mixed. The subsidiary recognizes no gain or loss on distributions to an 80-percent distributee.[3] For purposes of this rule, an 80-percent distributee is a parent corporation that meets the 80-percent stock ownership test of IRC Section 332 (b). On distributions to minority shareholders, the subsidiary recognizes gain[4] and not loss.[5]

The percentage ownership of a controlling corporation is determined as of the date of the adoption of the plan of liquidation. This date is the date when a resolution authorizing the liquidation is formally adopted by the corporation's shareholders.[6] In the case of a closely held corporation, however, the date that the plan is adopted is not necessarily the date of the adoption of a formal resolution authorizing the distribution of the firm's assets. In this case, the Internal Revenue Service will accept the date on which the holders of shares having sufficient voting power to authorize dissolution under state law make an informal agreement to liquidate.[7] A special rule permits the 80-percent distributee to include in its ownership percentage as of the date of adoption of the plan any stock in the subsidiary that is: (1) purchased by the 80-percent distributee for cash after the adoption of the plan of liquidation or (2) redeemed for cash by the subsidiary in the liquidation. Stock is not eligible for this rule, however, if it is redeemed for cash following a qualified Section 332 liquidation.

Another exception to the general rule requiring recognition of gain or loss on distributions in liquidations applies to tax-free reorganizations and distributions. According to IRC Sections 351 through 368 related to corporate reorganizations and distributions, there is nonrecognition on the gain or loss associated with the exchange or distribution of property.[8] For example, no gain is recognized on stock or securities of the controlled subsidiary distributed to shareholders in a split-up under Section 355. However, to the extent that a liquidating distribution pursuant to a reorganization includes appreciated property constituting boot, gain or loss is recognized.

Additional rules apply to subsidiary liquidations involving tax-exempt distributees and foreign distributees. The subsidiary recognizes all the gain inherent in its assets on the distribution of property to an 80-percent distributee that is a tax-exempt organization,[9] unless the property is used by the distributee in a trade or business unrelated to its tax-exempt purpose and is subject to tax under IRC Section 511.[10]

The nonrecognition treatment for liquidating distributions to domestic 80-percent distributees is not available for distributions to 80-percent distributees that are foreign corporations. The reason is that if a domestic corporation could distribute all its assets to its foreign parent without tax, the Internal Revenue Service might never receive any tax on the gain inherent in the assets.

FILING REQUIREMENTS FOR
THE LIQUIDATING FIRM

Prior to the Tax Reform Act of 1986, the liquidating firm had to file Form 966 (Corporate Dissolution or Liquidation) within thirty days after the adoption of a plan of complete liquidation. A certified copy of the plan of liquidation had to be attached to this form. An example of this certification is shown in Table 4.1. The corporation was also required to file Form 1096, a transmittal form, together with Form 1099L, which shows the amounts to be distributed to the shareholders in liquidation of the corporation. These two forms had to be filed on or before February 28 of the year following the calendar year in which the distribution was made.[11] The corporation also had to file its final tax return on or before the fifteenth day of the third month following the liquidation of the corporation.[12] In addition, the following information had to be attached to the return.[13]

1. A copy of the minutes of the stockholders' meeting at which the plan of liquidation was formally adopted including a copy of the plan of liquidation.

Table 4.1

An Example of Certification to Be Attached to Form 966 for Liquidating Firms

CERTIFICATION

I, B, Secretary of the XYZ Corporation, do hereby certify that the following is a true and correct copy of a PLAN OF COMPLETE LIQUIDATION UNDER SECTION 337 adopted by resolution at a joint directors' and shareholders' meeting of the XYZ Corporation held on the 12th day of February, 1976.

"PLAN OF COMPLETE LIQUIDATION UNDER SECTION 337

A. The officers of this corporation are hereby authorized to enter into negotiations and execute an agreement of sale, and to sell to the DEF Corporation the corporation's inventory and machinery and equipment, for a total price of $325,000. The officers of this corporation are further authorized to prepare and execute any and all papers and documents necessary or appropriate to carry out this resolution, including the power to execute bills of sale.

B. Resolved further that upon the sale of the corporate inventory and machinery and equipment, the corporation shall cease all manufacturing operations, and wind up its business. The corporation shall proceed to collect its receivable and pay its payables, including payment of the outstanding bank loan.

C. Resolved further that upon receipt of all receivables, and payment of all debts, the corporation shall distribute its remaining assets, which are to consist of cash, to its shareholders, in exchange for the 100 shares of stock held by them, in complete liquidation of this corporation.

D. Resolved further that the officers of this corporation are hereby empowered to take such action as is necessary to effectuate this plan of complete liquidation and liquidation of the corporation, including without limitation the execution and filing of the Certificate of Dissolution with the appropriate State authorities, and the preparation and filing with the Internal Revenue Service of any papers or documents which may be necessary or appropriate.

E. The sale of the corporate assets and the complete dissolution of this corporation are to occur as soon as practicable, but in no event later than twelve months from the date hereof, it being the intention of this corporation to qualify this liquidation under Section 337 of the Internal Revenue Code of 1954, as amended; and the officers of this corporation are authorized to take any and all necessary or appropriate action to qualify the liquidation under said Section 337 of the Internal Revenue Code."

IN WITNESS WHEREOF, my signature and the seal of the XYZ corporation has been affixed at the City of_____ County of_____ State of_____ this 20th day of February, 1976.

_____
Secretary

(Seal of Corporation)

Source: Stanley Hagendorf, *Tax Manual for Corporate Liquidations, Redemptions, and Estate Planning Recapitalizations* (Prentice-Hall, Inc., 1978, Englewood Cliffs, N.J.), pages 91–92, reprinted with permission from Garland Publications.

2. A statement of the assets sold after the adoption of the plan of liquidation, including the dates of such sales.

3. Information as to the date of the final liquidation distribution.

4. A statement of the assets, if any, retained to pay liabilities, and the nature of the liabilities.

It remains to be seen whether these filing requirements will be adhered to by the Internal Revenue Service or if new regulations governing filing requirements will be promulgated.

TAXATION OF STOCKHOLDERS

If the corporation sells its assets and distributes the sales proceeds in complete liquidation, the shareholder will report gain or loss based upon the difference between the sales proceeds distributed and the stockholder's tax basis in the stock. IRC Section 331 provides that in complete liquidation of corporations, the amounts distributed are treated as full payment in exchange for the stock. The amounts distributed in partial liquidations are treated as part or full payment in exchange for the stock.

The basis of assets received by a stockholder as a liquidating distribution is governed by IRC Section 334 (a), which provides that the basis of property received by the distributee shall be the fair market value of such property at the time of distribution. The stockholder is required to report gain or loss on the distribution on a personal income tax return in the same manner as if the stock were sold.

OTHER TAX FACTORS IN LIQUIDATIONS

Other tax factors in complete liquidations under IRC Section 337 include depreciation recapture, treatment of inventory, liquidation expenses, and deemed sale of assets in liquidation. If a corporation sells depreciable personal property at a gain, depreciation on the personal property is subject to recapture under Section 1245. Recapture means the firm recognizes ordinary income on the sale. Similarly, depreciation on real property including buildings may be recaptured under Section 1250.[14] IRC Section 336 (a) provides that a corporation generally recognizes losses when it distributes depreciated property in a complete liquidation. There are three exceptions to this rule. One of these exceptions relates to 80-percent distributees while the other two relate to potential tax avoidance cases.[15]

Gain or loss is recognized on the sale of inventory and property held for sale in the ordinary course of business and on installment obligations arising from such transactions. Prior to the Tax Reform Act of 1986, an exception was that if inventory and property held for sale were sold in a bulk sale to one buyer in one transaction, then no gain or loss was recognized on the sale. Additionally, Section 337 (f) requires recognition of income if LIFO (Last-in-First-out) inventory exceeds FIFO (First-in-First-out) inventory when the inventory is sold or exchanged with a third party.

Expenses related to the sale of assets in an IRC Section 337 liquidation such as legal and accounting fees and brokerage commissions are offset against the selling price of the assets and are not deductible against the corporate operating income. The reason is that the Internal Revenue Service maintains that since these expenses are attributable to the sale of assets, they are not deductible as ordinary liquidating expenses.

According to IRC Section 338, a corporation that buys at least 80 percent of the stock of a target corporation can elect to have the target corporation adjust the basis of its assets. IRC Section 338 (a) (1) treats the target corporation as having sold all its assets at fair market value in a fully taxable transaction. Under prior law, IRC Section 338 (a) (1) did not recognize gain or loss on the deemed sale except for recapture items because the sale was treated as occurring under former IRC Section 337. The Tax Reform Act of 1986 changes the treatment of the deemed sale so that gain is generally recognized. Since the purchasing corporation bears the economic burden of that tax, that corporation will seek to pay less for a target corporation to compensate for the potential tax liability.[16]

NOTES

1. See CCH Special 23, *Tax Reform Act of 1986, Law and Controlling Committee Reports*, vol. 72, no. 46, October 25, 1986, Commerce Clearing House, Inc., and CCH Special 22, *Explanation of Tax Reform Act of 1986*, vol. 73, no. 45, October 19, 1986, Commerce Clearing House, Inc.

2. IRC 337 (a) as amended by Act 631 (a).

3. IRC 337 (a).

4. IRC 336 (a).

5. IRC 336 (a) (3).

6. See Treasury Reg. Section 1.337–2 (b).

7. Rev. Rul. 65–235, 1965–2 C.B. 88.

8. IRC 336 (c).

9. IRC 337 (b) (2).

10. IRC 337 (b) (2) (B) (i).

11. IRC Section 6043.

12. IRC Section 6072.

13. Reg. Section 1.337–6.

14. Douglas H. Walter, "Unwanted Assets in Taxable and Tax-Free Corporate Acquisitions: Old Wine in New Bottles," *Taxes*, December, 1985, pp. 897–915.

15. James S. Eustice, Joel D. Kuntz, Charles S. Lewis, III, and Thomas P. Deering, *The Tax Reform Act of 1986, Analysis and Commentary* (Boston: Warren, Gorhan & Lamont, Inc., 1987), pp. 2-17–2-21.

16. Ibid., pp. 2-22–2-24.

5
Economic Analysis of Liquidations

This chapter analyzes the economic effects of voluntary corporate liquidations. Voluntary corporate liquidations result in significant wealth increases for common stockholders in the liquidating firms. Typically the liquidation proceeds distributed to shareholders exceed the market value of their shares. Although there have been several studies of corporate divestitures, very little systematic research on voluntary corporate liquidations has been conducted. The next section provides background information on corporate divestitures. Subsequent sections review the available literature dealing with voluntary corporate liquidations.

BACKGROUND

In recent years, a wave of corporate restructuring has occurred in the United States. This restructuring has taken many forms, including acquisitions, mergers, spin-offs, sell-offs, cut-backs, leveraged buy-outs, friendly and hostile takeovers, and liquidations. Proponents of the restructuring see it as a way of making American corporations more productive and competitive. This corporate restructuring is a response to various forces that have had an impact on the American economy in recent years.

One of the major factors driving the restructuring is intense foreign competition. Many American industries have suffered from heavy imports. Notable examples include the steel, automobile, and electronics industries. Another major factor has been the actions of

investment bankers and corporate raiders who are adept at identifying undervalued companies. These companies were not being
managed efficiently for the benefit of the common stockholders.
Eventually American corporate executives began to realize that big
is not necessarily better. Large American corporations had built en-
terprise-stifling bureaucracies that consisted of redundant layers of
management.[1] These companies lost the ability to quickly respond
to rapidly changing economic and competitive environments. Capital markets became more volatile in the 1970s, and inflation caused
the cost of capital to rise dramatically. All of these factors combined
to make companies unprofitable and to prevent them from achieving their targeted financial objectives. Corporate restructuring
emerged as a response to these factors.

One type of restructuring that has occurred with increased fre-
quency in recent years is corporate divestitures. Several studies have
been conducted in recent years on voluntary corporate divestitures.
The two forms of divestiture that have been examined are spin-offs
and sell-offs.[2] A spin-off involves the pro-rata distribution of all the
common stock of a subsidiary to the parent firm's stockholders so
that after the spin-off there are two separate publicly owned firms.
A sell-off occurs when a firm sells some of its assets for cash but
continues to exist as a going concern. Most of the voluntary corporate divestiture studies found that the announcement of a spin-
off or sell-off had a significant positive impact on the returns of the
common stockholders of the parent corporation.

Another form of voluntary divestiture that has received limited
attention is complete corporate liquidation. A complete corporate
liquidation occurs when the firm sells substantially all of its assets,
distributes the liquidation proceeds to its common stockholders, and
ceases an independent existence. Liquidations differ from sell-offs
in that the liquidating firm ceases an independent existence, whereas
in sell-offs the selling firm remains as a going concern. Although
the financial press has tracked several firms that have voluntarily
liquidated in recent years, surprisingly little research has been conducted.[3] The empirical studies dealing exclusively with voluntary
corporate liquidations were conducted by Skantz and Marchesini
(1987), Kudla (1987), and Kim and Schatzberg (1987). The next
sections discuss these studies.

THE SKANTZ AND MARCHESINI STUDY

Skantz and Marchesini analyzed the shareholder wealth effects of thirty-seven firms that voluntarily liquidated during the 1970 to 1982 period. They found that the liquidation announcement resulted in significant positive risk-adjusted shareholder returns. To measure risk-adjusted shareholder returns, Skantz and Marchesini used the market model methodology developed by Fama, Fisher, Jensen, and Roll (1969). The advantage of this technique is that it is an automatic control for both movements in the stock market during the period surrounding the liquidation announcement date and for differential risk associated with each firm. The primary control for the market effect comes from netting out the return on the market. Market effects are also controlled to some extent by averaging over widely disparate time periods.

Residuals were estimated from Equation 1:

$$\tilde{R}_{jt} = a_j + b_j \tilde{R}_{mt} + e_{jt} \tag{1}$$

where $\tilde{R}_{jt}$ is the return on security j in month t consisting of capital gains yield and dividend yield adjusted for stock splits and stock dividends; a_j and b_j are parameters to be estimated by least squares; $\tilde{R}_{mt}$ is University of Chicago's Center for Research on Security Prices (CRSP) equally weighted monthly index of New York Stock Exchange firms; and e_{jt} is the residual return on security j for month t; and the tildes indicate random variables. The analysis focuses on e_{jt} because the residual return represents that portion of the security's monthly return which is not related to the return on the market. These residuals were examined to determine whether or not they were affected by the liquidation announcement.

The parameters a_j and b_j were estimated by regressing security returns on market returns as described in Equation 1 for months $t = -71$ to $t = -12$ (where $t = 0$ is the announcement month). The risk-adjusted return of each stock is found for $t = -11$ to $t = 0$ by calculating the residual return, e_{jt} as follows:

$$e_{jt} = R_{jt} - (a_j + b_j R_{mt}) \tag{2}$$

The monthly residuals for the thirty-seven firms were averaged in an attempt to avoid the effects of other firm-specific events, which might have influenced a particular firm's monthly residual returns. A positive residual for any week indicates performance greater than expected given the risk class of the firm and the return on the market; a negative residual indicates performance less than expected given the risk class of the firm and the return on the market. Monthly average residuals for the month m were defined as follows:

$$e_m = \frac{\sum\limits_{j=1}^{37} e_{jm}}{37} \quad m = -11 \text{ to } 0 \tag{3}$$

The cumulative residuals for each month were computed from the monthly average residuals as follows:

$$E_M = \sum_{j=-11}^{M} \bar{e}_j \quad M = -11 \text{ to } 0 \tag{4}$$

If there is no market reaction to the liquidation announcement, then E_M would be expected to fluctuate randomly about zero. Positive cumulative residuals imply performance of the liquidating firm's shares is "in excess" of expectations given the risk class of the firm and the movement of the market; negative cumulative residuals indicate performance is less than expected given the risk class of the firm and the movement of the market. Note that a "favorable" price movement is defined relative to the market. Thus, if the market goes down and the stock goes down, this could be a favorable movement as long as the stock went down less than expected.

Other things being equal, the market's reaction is expected to result in a positive impact on stock prices (i.e., positive returns) for the reasons given in Chapter 2. The results of the analysis are shown in Table 5.1. As shown in Table 5.1, the residual returns, both average and cumulative, begin a systematic deviation from zero about five to seven months prior to the announcement. This result suggests that the liquidation announcements are anticipated by the market. The average excess return was 21.4 percent in the announcement month and cumulative excess return was 41.3 percent in the twelve-month period prior to the announcement. Both of these values are highly significant as indicated by the Z-statistics. Accordingly, shareholders realized significantly positive risk-adjusted returns due to the liquidation decision.

Table 5.1
Average and Cumulative Average Excess Returns for Liquidating Firms

	AVERAGE		CUMULATIVE AVERAGE	
TIME	VALUE	Z-STATISTIC	VALUE	Z-STATISTIC
-11	-0.0206	-1.805	-0.0206	-1.805
-10	0.0057	0.215	-0.0149	-1.124
-9	0.0206	1.125	0.0056	-0.268
-8	0.0311	1.284	0.0368	0.409
-7	0.0349	1.943	0.0718	1.235
-6	0.0212	1.170	0.0930	1.605
-5	0.0448	2.211	0.1379	2.322
-4	-0.0029	0.098	0.1349	2.207
-3	0.0139	2.339	0.1488	2.860
-2	-0.0133	-0.463	0.1355	2.567
-1	0.0633	2.724	0.1988	3.269
0	0.2145	11.450	0.4133	6.435

Source: "The Effect of Voluntary Corporate Liquidation on Shareholder Wealth, by Terrance R. Skantz and Roberto Marchesini," *Journal of Financial Research* 10, no. 1, Spring 1987, page 72, reprinted with permission.

Skantz and Marchesini identified three possible sources of these excess returns. First, the assets may be worth more to the buyer than to the seller and, therefore, the buyer is willing to pay a premium, or more than the liquidating firm's going concern value, to acquire the assets. Second, any diseconomies associated with excessive diversification can be eliminated by piecemeal sale of the firm's assets in liquidation. Finally, and most importantly, there was favorable tax treatment on the gains from the sale of corporate assets. Under Section 337 of the Internal Revenue Code of 1954, any gain or loss on the sale or exchange of a company's assets is non-taxable to the company provided that the company adopts a plan of complete liquidation prior to the sale of its assets and that thereafter all of the company's assets, except those retained to meet claims against the company, are fully distributed to shareholders within one year of adoption of the plan.[4]

THE KUDLA STUDY

Kudla sought to explain the excess returns accruing to shareholders in liquidating firms by focusing on the role of corporate insiders.[5] Kudla hypothesized that reaching consensus on the board of directors for the liquidation decision is greatly facilitated by the existence of corporate insiders who own a significant amount of the company's common stock. Insiders who have a controlling interest or significant ownership interest can exert considerable influence on the board of directors in any policy decision, including the liquidation decision.[6] This agreement is less likely in firms that do not have significant insider ownership. This hypothesized relationship may partially explain why some publicly traded firms liquidate while most do not.

There are several reasons why insiders may view complete corporate liquidation as in the best interests of all stockholders. All stockholders benefit from the liquidation because the liquidation proceeds to be distributed to stockholders typically exceed the market value of their stock based on past trading of such stock when there was no merger or liquidation activity.[7] However, insiders realize a larger dollar increase in their wealth because they own a larger fraction of the firm's outstanding shares.[8] They therefore have a greater incentive to find a buyer willing to pay a premium for the firm's assets. Furthermore, if there is an illiquid market for the company's shares, liquidation gives insiders who are large stockholders the opportunity to diversify their investments while all stockholders have the opportunity to receive cash for their investments.[9] For these reasons, the increase in market value of the common stock associated with the liquidation announcement is hypothesized to be significantly and positively related to the fraction of outstanding shares held by insiders.

Another way that insiders can benefit from information related to the liquidation decision is by engaging in short-term insider trading. However, insider trading is regulated by the Securities and Exchange Act of 1934. Insiders can be sued for violating their fiducial responsibilities to their shareholders if they trade on material nonpublic information prior to the public announcement of the information.[10] However, the decision to trade or not would also depend on the expected costs.

Although insiders might trade for their own account based on inside information concerning the liquidation decision, they can also benefit via an increase in the value of their stock options. Insiders who own significant amounts of stock options have a greater incentive to find a buyer willing to pay a premium for the firm's assets because they have more to gain. Accordingly, the increase in shareholder wealth arising from the liquidation announcement should be a positive function of the number of stock options held by insiders.

The sample for Kudla's study consisted of twenty-five firms that liquidated in the 1970 to 1982 period.[11] The liquidation announcement dates were obtained from the *Wall Street Journal* and the proxy statements for the liquidating firms. Linear regression analysis is used to test the hypotheses concerning insiders. The linear first-order regression model has the following basic form:

$$R = A_0 + A_1[H] + A_2[O] + A_3[B] + A_4[S] + e \qquad (5)$$

where R is the two-day total return on the common stock consisting of the return the day before and the day of the liquidation announcement; H is the fraction of outstanding common stock shares held by insiders; O is the number of unexercised options held by insiders divided by the number of outstanding common stock shares; B is the number of shares purchased by insiders in the year prior to the liquidation announcement divided by the number of outstanding common stock shares; S is the number of shares sold by insiders in the year prior to the liquidation announcement divided by the number of outstanding common stock shares; and e is the random error term.

Since it was impossible to tell if the firm actually made the liquidation announcement before or after the close of trading on the day preceding the announcement, returns for the day before the announcement and the day of the announcement were summed and analyzed for each sample firm.[12] The time frame selected for measuring insider trading activity, B and S, was one year prior to the announcement date because a number of the liquidating firms were in negotiations with one or more potential purchasers of the firm's assets for several months prior to the event. Typically there was uncertainty in the market as to the identity of the potential purchasers and whether or not the negotiations would be successful. Accordingly, information leakage was expected and the effect on the common stock price was expected to be spread out over time.

The prices of the common stock were obtained from *Standard and Poor's Daily Stock Price Record*. The data on insider trading activity were obtained from the *Securities and Exchange Commission Official Summary of Security Transactions and Holdings*. The insider holdings and the number of unexercised options were obtained from the proxy statements for the liquidating firms.

Standard t-tests from the regression analysis are used to deter-

Table 5.2
Descriptive Statistics for the Variables Used in the Regression Analysis (Percent)

Variable	Mean	Standard Deviation	Maximum	Minimum	N
R	8.2	10.9	41.7	-10.9	25
H	22.6	21.1	72.9	1.6	25
O	1.8	1.6	7.2	.1	24
B	2.3	4.8	19.0	0.0	22
S	2.4	7.9	37.0	0.0	22

R = two-day return in percent for the day prior to and day of the liquidation announcement.

H = the fraction of outstanding common stock shares held by insiders expressed as a percent.

O = number of unexercised options held by insiders expressed as a percent of the number of outstanding common stock shares.

B = the number of shares purchased by insiders in the year prior to the liquidation announcement expressed as a percent of the number of outstanding common stock shares.

S = the number of shares sold by insiders in the year prior to the liquidation announcement expressed as a percent of the number of outstanding common stock shares.

mine the significance of the regression coefficients. The signs of these variables are also examined to determine if the explanatory variables are acting in the intended direction. The coefficients for H and O are predicted to be positive and significant, while the signs and significance of the coefficients for B and S depend on the insiders' decision to trade or not.

Descriptive statistics for the variables are shown in Table 5.2. Note that the mean value of R of 8.2 percent was substantial. A total of 21 of the 25 R values were positive. Based on a test of proportions and assuming that positive and negative returns are

Table 5.3
Regression Analysis Results (T-Statistics in Parentheses)

Regression Number	Independent Variables					R^2	F	N
	A_0	H	O	B	S			
1	.037 (1.21)	.20 (2.02)*				.15	4.08*	25
2	.049 (1.01)		2.03 (1.00)			.04	1.00	24
3	.062 (1.84)			−.63 (−.97)		.04	.94	22
4	.036 (1.15)				.52 (1.33)	.08	1.78	22
5	.049 (1.40)			−.54 (−.84)	.48 (1.22)	.11	1.23	22

*Significant at the .05 level with a one-tailed test

equally likely, the chi-square statistic for R with one degree of freedom was 11.56, which is significant at the 1 percent level. Accordingly, we reject the hypothesis that the proportions of positive and negative returns are equal. Note also that the mean value of the fraction of insider holdings was 22.6 percent with a range of 1.6 to 72.9 percent, indicating considerable sample variance. The proportion of unexercised stock options held by insiders was a relatively low 1.8 percent. As evidenced by the mean values for B and S, the levels of buying and selling activity by insiders in the one-year period prior to the liquidation announcement were similar.

The regression results are shown in Table 5.3. The statistically significant F-values in Table 5.3 indicate the presence of linear regression. Most of the R^2s are low, but it must be emphasized that total explanatory power was not an issue in this study. What was paramount was the size, sign, and statistical significance of the independent variables.

As predicted, the fraction of insider holdings as measured by H was significant and positive in regression number 1. This result implies that larger equity holdings by insiders are associated with greater increases in shareholder wealth. One possible explanation for this result is that insiders have a greater incentive to search for a buyer who is willing to pay a premium for the liquidating firm's assets if the insiders have more wealth to gain.

The coefficient for the number of unexercised options (0) in Table 5.3 was positive as predicted but insignificant probably because insiders did not hold large amounts of stock options as shown in Table 5.2. There was no evidence of significant insider trading activity prior to the liquidation announcement as evidenced by the insignificance of the coefficients for the B and S variables as shown in regression numbers 3, 4, and 5.

THE KIM AND SCHATZBERG STUDY

Kim and Schatzberg examined the possible motives for and consequences of seventy-three voluntary corporate liquidations that occurred from 1963 to 1982. Using daily returns and the residual methodology, which was described in the Skantz and Marchesini study, Kim and Schatzberg found that the liquidation announcements were associated with significant gains to shareholders of the liquidating firms. According to Kim and Schatzberg, this finding suggests that the assets of the liquidating firms were underutilized prior to the liquidations and that voluntary liquidations lead to higher valued reallocations of corporate resources.

One possible motive for these excess returns explored by Kim and Schatzberg was a transfer of wealth from bondholders to stockholders. Specifically, if the selling firm in liquidation retires debt at face value when the market value of the debt is substantially higher than its face value, wealth transfers from bondholders to stockholders will occur. The empirical evidence, however, indicated that the market value of outstanding debt for forty-nine of the liquidating firms was less than the average book value of the debt, resulting in an additional cost to the liquidating firms' stockholders.

An analysis of twenty-six potential acquirers of liquidating firms indicated no significant effects on shareholder wealth. All the gains of liquidation appear to accrue to stockholders of the selling firm. Accordingly, Kim and Schatzberg concluded that the market for corporate acquisitions is highly competitive on the buyers' side.

This chapter reviewed three studies on voluntary corporate liquidations. These studies indicated that the liquidation decision increased the wealth of the common stockholders in the liquidating firms. In other words, these firms were worth more dead than alive.

The decision to liquidate appears to be motivated by tax factors and by the influence of corporate insiders.

NOTES

See References section at the end of this chapter for full bibliographic information concerning studies.

1. See "Restructuring Really Works," *Fortune Magazine*, March 2, 1987, pp. 38–46.

2. Studies of spin-offs include Hite and Owers (1983), Kudla and McInish (1983), Miles and Rosenfeld (1983), Rosenfeld (1984), and Schipper and Smith (1983). Sell-offs were analyzed by Alexander, Benson, and Kampmeyer (1984), Boudreaux (1975), Klein (1983), Hearth and Zaima (1984), and Jain (1985).

3. See, for example, *Business Week*, July 26, 1976, p. 109; November 7, 1977, p. 26; and October 2, 1978, p. 36.

4. This tax advantage has been largely eliminated by the Tax Reform Act of 1986, which requires that the gains on the sale of a liquidating firm's assets be treated as taxable to the firm. The likely effects of this change in tax laws will be the discouragement of future liquidations motivated mainly by tax factors, a requirement for the liquidating firm to receive a higher premium for its assets, the provision of incentive for liquidating firms to restructure their business organizations through such venues as limited partnerships, and the creation of more important motives for liquidation.

5. Individuals who are officers, directors, and owners of 10 percent or more of any equity class of securities are defined as insiders by the Securities and Exchange Act of 1934.

6. Evidence that managerial welfare affects policy decisions was reported by Larcker and Balkcom (1983), Walkling and Long (1984), and Lewellen, Loderer, and Rosenfeld (1985).

7. It follows that there is no conflict between insiders and outside equity holders. In addition, a majority of stockholders approved the plan of complete liquidation in each of the sample firms examined in the study.

8. Although insiders lose their jobs in liquidation, the value of their salaries was a relatively small 3.5 percent of the value of their common stockholdings for the sample of twenty-five firms used in this study.

9. One measure of liquidity is if the stock trades every day. A visual inspection of the volume data in a three-month period prior to the liquidation announcement indicated that more than half of the sample firms did not trade continuously or they traded at a low volume.

10. Section 10 of the Securities and Exchange Act of 1934 prohibits fraud in the purchase or sale of securities. Section 16 (a) requires the re-

porting of insiders' transactions. Section 16 (b) requires the profits from purchases and sales within six months of each other to be returned to the corporation. Section 16 (c) prohibits short sales by insiders. Section 32 as amended in 1975 provides penalties of up to $10,000 in fines and five years of imprisonment for violating any provision of the securities law.

11. These twenty-five firms were included in the sample of thirty-seven firms that was examined by Skantz and Marchesini (1987). The other twelve firms were excluded from this study because of missing or incomplete data. This data was necessary to test the hypotheses.

12. The market-adjusted-returns model described by Brown and Warner (1985) was also used in this study, but the results were essentially the same as reported here. In this model, the abnormal return was calculated as, $E_{jt} = R_{jt} - R_{mt}$ where R_{mt} was based on the *Standand and Poor's 500 Index*.

REFERENCES

Alexander, G., G. Benson, and J. Kampmeyer. "Investigating the Valuation Effects of Announcements of Voluntary Corporate Selloffs," *Journal of Finance* 39 (June 1984):503–517.

Boudreaux, K. "Divestiture and Share Price," *Journal of Financial and Quantitative Analysis* 10 (November 1975):619–626.

Brown, S. J., and J. B. Warner. "Using Daily Stock Returns," *Journal of Financial Economics* (1985):3–31.

Fama, E. F., Lawrence Fisher, Michael C. Jensen, and Richard Roll. "The Adjustment of Stock Prices to New Information," *International Economic Review* 10, no. 1 (February 1969):1–21.

Hearth, D., and J. Zaima. "Voluntary Corporate Divestitures and Value," *Financial Management* (Spring 1984):10–16.

Hite, G., and J. Owers. "Security Price Reaction around Corporate Spinoff Announcements," *Journal of Financial Economics* (December 1983):409–436.

Jain, P. "The Effect of Voluntary Selloff Announcements on Shareholder Wealth," *Journal of Finance* (March 1985):209–224.

Han Kim, E., and J. D. Schatzberg. "Voluntary Corporate Liquidations," *Journal of Financial Economics* (May 1987).

Klein, A. "Voluntary Corporate Divestitures: Motives and Consequences," unpublished Ph.D. dissertation, June 1983, University of Chicago.

Kudla, R. "Corporate Insiders and the Liquidation Decision," unpublished manuscript, University of Wisconsin–Eau Claire, 1987.

Kudla, R., and T. McInish. "Valuation Consequences of Corporate Spin-offs," *Review of Business and Economic Research* 18 (March 1983):71–177.

Larcker, O. F., and J. E. Balkcom. "Executive Compensation Contracts and Investment Behavior: An Analysis of Mergers," unpublished manuscript, Northwestern University, Evanston, Illinois, 1983.

Lewellen, W., C. Loderer, and A. Rosenfeld. "Merger Decisions and Executive Stock Ownership in Acquiring Firms," *Journal of Accounting and Economics* (1985):209–231.

Miles, J., and J. Rosenfeld. "The Effect of Spinoff Announcements on Shareholder Wealth," *Journal of Finance* 38 (December 1983):1597–1606.

Rosenfeld, J. "Additional Evidence on the Relation between Divestiture Announcements and Shareholder Wealth," *Journal of Finance* (December 1984):1437–1448.

Schipper, K., and A. Smith. "Effects of Recontracting on Shareholder Wealth: The Case of Voluntary Spin-Offs," *Journal of Financial Economics* 12 (December 1983):437–468.

Skantz, T., and R. Marchesini. "The Effect of Voluntary Corporate Liquidation on Shareholder Wealth," *Journal of Financial Research* (Spring 1987):65–75.

Walkling, R. A., and M. S. Long. "Agency Theory, Managerial Welfare, and Takeover Bid Resistance," *Rand (Bell) Journal of Economics* 15 (1984):54–68.

6

Case Studies

This chapter reviews the circumstances surrounding three large voluntary corporate liquidations. These liquidated firms are Kaiser Industries Corporation, UV Industries, Inc., and Tishman Realty and Construction Company, Inc. These firms were selected for analysis because they exhibit the diversity of liquidation scenarios and there was sufficient publicly available information to examine them.

KAISER INDUSTRIES CORPORATION

The liquidation of Kaiser Industries Corporation (KIC) was one of the largest liquidations of a family owned company in American history.[1] The principal assets of KIC were controlling interests in Kaiser Steel Corporation, Kaiser Aluminum and Chemical, and Kaiser Cement and Gypsum. These stocks represented approximately 70 percent of KIC's total assets in 1976. KIC also owned Kaiser Broadcasting, Kaiser Aerospace and Electronics, Kaiser Engineers, and Kaiser Sand and Gravel. The consolidated balance sheet and statement of net earnings for Kaiser Industries Corporation and its subsidiaries are shown as Tables 6.1 and 6.2, respectively.

Kaiser Steel Corporation was engaged in the production and sale of iron and steel and related products from western United States mines and plants. Kaiser Steel was also engaged in ocean transportation through a wholly owned subsidiary, Kaiser International Shipping Corporation; had a 32.6 percent interest in Kaiser Resources Ltd., which was principally engaged in the extraction, pro-

Table 6.1
Consolidated Balance Sheets for Kaiser Industries Corporation and Its Subsidiaries for Year Ended December 31, 1976 (Thousands of Dollars)

	Kaiser Industries and Consolidated Subsidiaries	Adjustments to Show Kaiser Steel as an Unconsolidated Company[A]	Kaiser Industries and Subsidiaries with Kaiser Steel at Equity
Current Assets			
Cash	$134,676	$ (69,304)	$ 65,372
Receivables	108,872	(53,876)	54,996
Inventories	118,094	(102,129)	15,965
Other current assets	38,293	(25,791)	12,502
Total	$399,935	(251,100)	$148,835
Investments			
Kaiser Aluminum common stock	278,702	---	278,702
Kaiser Steel common stock	---	262,475	262,473
Kaiser Cement common stock	32,918		32,918
Other	181,929	(155,340)	26,589
Total	$493,549	107,135	$600,684
Property, plant and equipment-net	$501,150	(450,259)	50,891
Other assets	37,238	(12,920)	24,318
Total assets	$1,431,872	$(607,144)	$824,728

cessing, and export of metallurgical coal in Canada; and had a 28.3 percent in Hamersley Holdings Ltd., which was involved in the mining and exporting of iron ore and pellets in Australia.

Kaiser Aluminum and Chemical was the third largest domestic producer of primary aluminum and fabricated aluminum products. Its aluminum operations included the mining of bauxite, the production of alumina from bauxite, the reduction of alumina to aluminum, and the fabrication of aluminum and aluminum alloys into a variety of products. Kaiser Aluminum and Chemical had substantial interests in aluminum operations in Africa, Asia, Australia, New

Table 6.1 (continued)

	Kaiser Industries and Consolidated Subsidiaries	Adjustments to Show Kaiser Steel as an Unconsolidated Company[A]	Kaiser Industries and Subsidiaries with Kaiser Steel at Equity
Current liabilities			
Notes payable and current debt	$24,523	$ (13,941)	$ 10,582
Accounts payable	36,432	(22,613)	13,819
Payroll liabilities	69,225	(50,205)	19,020
Income taxes	32,415	(23,160)	9,255
Other current liabilities	46,674	(21,591)	25,083
Total	209,269	(131,510)	77,759
Long-term debt	198,193	(172,510)	25,819
Deferred income taxes	111,307	(80,262)	31,045
Minority interest	227,712	(222,998)	4,714
Stockholders' equity	685,391		685,391
Total liabilities and stockholders' equity	$1,431,872	$(607,144)	$824,728

[A] To eliminate the accounts of Kaiser Steel and to reflect Kaiser Industries's investment in Kaiser Steel by the equity method.

Source: Kaiser Industries Corporation's proxy statement, March 21, 1977, page 6.

Zealand, Canada, Europe, and Jamaica. The company also produced agricultural chemicals, refractories, and industrial chemicals, engaged in international commodity trading, and had investments in real estate.

Kaiser Cement and Gypsum produced and marketed portland cement and gypsum products in the western United States and Hawaii. It also owned and operated a cement plant in Texas, produced insulating board and boxboard paper, sold aggregates and ready mix concrete, and engaged in limited real estate activities.

There were several reasons that the board of directors of KIC decided to liquidate the firm. One of the major reasons was that KIC's common stock had traditionally traded at a substantial discount from the combined market value of its common stock stock-

Table 6.2
Consolidated Statement of Net Earnings for Kaiser Industries Corporation and Its Subsidiaries for Year Ended December 31, 1976 (Thousands of Dollars)

	Kaiser Industries and Consolidated Subsidiaries	Adjustments to Show Kaiser Steel as an Unconsolidated Company[A]	Kaiser Industries and Subsidiaries with Kaiser Steel at Equity
Net sales and operating revenues	$1,015,871	$(677,075)	$338,796
Other	29,659	(22,030)	7,629
	1,045,530	(699,105)	346,425
Costs and expenses			
Costs of products and services	860,350	(599,911)	260,439
Selling and administrative expense	94,295	(48,178)	46,117
Depreciation, depletion and amortization	44,175	(34,933)	9,242
Interest	15,093	(12,794)	2,299
Income taxes	3,711	8,165	11,876
	1,017,624	(687,651)	329,973
Earnings before equity of unconsolidated companies, minority interest, and extraordinary item	27,906	(11,454)	16.452
Equity in earnings of unconsolidated companies	52,060	(8,050)	44,010
Minority interest	(23,252)	19,504	(3,748)
Earnings before extraordinary item	56,714	--	56,714
Extraordinary tax credit	10,000	--	10,000
Net earnings	$ 66,714	$ --	$ 66,714

_____

[A] To eliminate the accounts of Kaiser Steel and to show Kaiser Industries' share of Kaiser Steel's earnings by the equity method.

Source: Kaiser Industries Corporation's proxy statement, March 21, 1977, page 10.

Table 6.3
Historical and Pro-Forma Market Prices for Kaiser Industries Corporation's Common Stock

	Pro Forma Portfolio Stocks Market Price	Historical Kaiser Industries Market Price	Discount (Premium)	Discount (Premium) Percentage
December 31,				
1972	$ 7.28	$ 5.88	$1.40	19%
1973	8.24	7.25	.99	12
1974	6.81	4.63	2.18	32
1975	12.42	8.50	3.92	32
1976	14.57	15.00	(.43)	(3)

Source: Kaiser Industries Corporation's Proxy Statement, March 21, 1977, page 4.

holdings in Kaiser Steel, Kaiser Aluminum, and Kaiser Cement, without considering the value of the firm's other net assets. Historical data on this discount are provided in Table 6.3.

The board of directors and management of KIC expect that by liquidating the firm and distributing to KIC's common stockholders the firm's common stockholdings in Kaiser Steel, Kaiser Aluminum, and Kaiser Cement, the firm's common stockholders will receive greater equity security value than would have been available to them through continued ownership of the firm's common stock had the plan of liquidation not been adopted and implemented. Accordingly, the basis for the historical discount would be eliminated.

Upon liquidation, each shareholder of Kaiser Industries' common stock owning 100 shares of KIC's stock would receive 13 shares of Kaiser Steel, 25 shares of Kaiser Aluminum, and 7 shares of Kaiser Cement. The liquidation should also result in an increased dividend yield because the cash dividends paid on KIC's common stock have been less than the cash dividends paid on a pro-rata share of the three portfolio stocks. The estimated liquidation values of KIC's assets is shown as Table 6.4.

The main reason that KIC's common stock traded at a discount from the combined market value of the three Kaiser common stocks in its portfolio was the continued losses by Kaiser Steel (the financial condition and performance of Kaiser Steel is shown in Tables 6.1 and 6.2). The poor performance of Kaiser Steel was due to sev-

Table 6.4
Estimated Liquidation Values of Kaiser Industries' Assets

Investments	Percent Ownership	Market Value (Million of Dollar)	Percent of Total Assets
Kaiser Aluminum & Chemical	37	$268.7	39.46
Kaiser Steel	56	126.8	25.0
Kaiser Cement & Gypsum	37	22.3	2.9
Natural Steel & Shipbuilding	50	17.1	2.7
Other		4.2	0.7
Wholly-owned operations			
Kaiser Sand & Gravel		39.1	6.2
Kaiser Broadcasting		42.6	5.8
Kaiser Engineers		30.5	5.3
Kaiser Aerospace		13.4	2.8
Other		57.4	9.2
Total		$622.1	100.0%

eral factors, including intense foreign competition mainly from Japan, exceptionally high labor and raw material costs, lack of fully modernized plant and equipment, and poorly located facilities. KIC had attempted to sell or merge Kaiser Steel, but these efforts were unsuccessful. Accordingly, liquidation was deemed to be advantageous.

UV INDUSTRIES, INC.

UV Industries, Inc., was the successor to United States Smelting Refining and Mining Company, which was acquired in 1964 by Martin Horwitz and associates after a two-year proxy fight.[2] Since 1964, the company grew rapidly primarily through acquisition such that in 1978 the company earned $42.5 million on sales of $594 million.

UV's principal asset was Federal Pacific Electric Company, a wholly owned subsidiary which was engaged in the design, manufacture, and sale of electrical control, distribution, and transmission equipment, including standard and specially designed low-voltage equipment, power equipment, and electronic components. For the years ended 1976 and 1977, Federal Pacific provided 47 percent and 42 percent of UV's assets, respectively, and 68 percent and 58 percent, respectively, of its operating profit. UV also owned copper, coal, and gold operations, oil and gas properties, and a lead-refining company.

Under the leadership of Martin Horwitz, Chairman of the Board of UV Industries, Inc., the company had grown to be one of the largest companies in the United States (number 357 on the *Fortune* 500 List). The company was financially sound and profitable. For these reasons, the capital markets were surprised when, at Horwitz's request, UV's directors unanimously approved a resolution that all the company's assets be sold or distributed to shareholders in complete liquidation. However, what appeared on the surface to be an irrational act was actually in the best interests of all of UV's common stockholdings.

Horwitz was frustrated by the fact that the company's stock had traded at a relatively low 2 to 6 times earnings since 1973 while analysts consistently valued UV's assets at more than twice the company's common stock value. But it was the proposed sale of Federal Pacific Electric Comany to a subsidiary of Reliance Electric Company for $345 million that first caused Horwitz to contemplate total liquidation. Prior to the company's decision to liquidate, the stock was selling for about $19 per share. After the liquidation plan was announced, the price jumped to about $30. Eventually, the market price exceeded $35 per share.

The decision to liquidate UV Industries was the result of a combination of circumstances that included the desire to avoid an unfriendly takeover by Victor Posner, Chairman of Sharon Steel Company, a specialty steel company; management's interest in putting the intrinsic value of the company's assets, which the stock market was ignoring, in the hands of the common stockholders; and the firm's need to escape a tax liability of $42 million on the sale of Federal Pacific.

Martin Horwitz's first contact with Victor Posner was in 1975 when UV was interested in selling Phoenix Steel, a company that Horwitz gained control of six years earlier. Posner's Sharon Steel was a potential buyer, but no agreement was reached. However, Horwitz said later, "While Posner was talking about the tomato patch, he started looking up at the main house." By June of 1976, Sharon Steel had acquired about 20 percent of UV's common stock. What alarmed Horwitz most was some warrants outstanding for the purchase of 3.8 million shares of common stock that were selling cheap. Horwitz was concerned that Posner might buy these warrants, exercise them, and take over the company. UV was exposed because the warrants had an expiration date of January 15, 1979.

In November, 1978, Reliance Electric offered $345 million for Federal Pacific. Horwitz felt that he could not refuse this offer because it reflected a price–earnings multiple of 13 to 14 at a time when UV's common stock was selling at a multiple of 5. This offer eliminated Horwitz's concern about losing control of the company because he knew that the warrants outstanding would be exercised. UV announced the sale of Federal Pacific on December 18, which was less than a month before the warrants expired. UV stock price quickly jumped above the exercise price of the warrants, guaranteeing that the warrants would be exercised. Moreover, the Hart-Scott-Rodimo Antitrust Improvement Act of 1976 requires any large shareholder to declare his intention of increasing his holdings in a company at least thirty days before he actually does so. Accordingly, Posner would have had to declare his intention to exercise any warrants before December 15 because the warrants expired on January 15. Since UV did not announce the sale of Federal Pacific until December 18, Posner had lost his opportunity to take over the company. Posner's ownership of UV had grown to 22 percent by January of 1979, but when warrant holders exercised their warrant due to the rise in stock price, Posner's interest was diluted to 13.5 percent.

The sale of Federal Pacific left UV with a huge capital gain and a tax liability of $42 million. To avoid this liability, Horwitz decided to liquidate the firm under Section 337 of the Internal Revenue Code. According to this code, any corporation that liquidates itself in one year pays no corporate capital gains tax on the sale of its assets. Other factors that UV's board of directors considered in making the liquidation decision included the possibility of a recession, continued inflation, depressed stock market prices, and risks inherent in an acquisition program.

TISHMAN REALTY AND CONSTRUCTION COMPANY, INC.

Tishman Realty and Construction Company, Inc., was one of the largest publicly held real estate companies engaged in the ownership and operation of commercial real estate properties.[3] Most of the office building projects in which the company owned interests were located in the metropolitan areas of New York city, Chicago, Cleveland, San Francisco, and Los Angeles. The company had assets of $260 million and gross revenues from properties in fiscal 1976 of $90 million.

The board of directors of the company concluded that it was in the best interests of the common stockholders to liquidate the company because they believed that shareholders would receive greater benefit from the sale of the company's assets than they would if the company continued in existence and the shareholders' only means of realizing the value of their investment was by selling the common stock in the stock market.

The main reason given by Tishman's management for the difference in the value of the company's assets and market value of its common stock is the accounting rule that requires assets to be carried on the books at historic cost minus depreciation even though they may have appreciated substantially and generated a large cash flow. For example, the company had on its books a group of sixteen office buildings at a value $3.7 million less than the $171 million in mortgages and other liabilities on them. But under the liquidation plan these buildings would be sold for $109.1 million in cash over the mortgages. Management believed that this disparity in book value and market value had confused investors and prevented the securities markets from properly valuing the company's assets.

Tishman's management had been studying the possibility of restructuring the company in a form that would be more beneficial to shareholders since 1973. With the assistance of Morgan Stanley & Company, the company developed a complex liquidation plan that involved selling most of its assets, which consisted primarily of twenty-four office buildings for $114 million in cash, and forming a partnership that would own whatever assets were not sold. The company would make an initial cash distribution to all of its stockholders totaling $71 million, equivalent to $11 a share, and give them limited partnership interests in the new organization proportionate to their stock holdings. The objective of the partnership is to sell the assets it acquired and to distribute the proceeds to the partners.

The advantages of the partnership include: (1) the ability of the partnership to make distributions to its partners from cash flow that is expected to be greater than the corporation's ability to pay dividends to its shareholders, (2) the partnership will not be subject to income tax, and (3) partnership distributions will receive more favorable tax treatment than will corporate dividends. Under New York law, a corporation may pay dividends only out of surplus, which is defined as the amount by which the net assets of the corporation exceed its stated capital. The corporation's financial statements had not shown a surplus since the end of its 1974 fiscal year. Accordingly, the corporation had been unable to pay any dividends since 1974. These surplus restrictions do not apply to the partnership. Therefore, the partnership anticipates distributing a substantial portion of its cash flow to the partners. In addition, the partners would be free of requirements for public disclosure.

NOTES

1. See "Kaiser Industries' Basic Dilemma," *Business Week*, May 24, 1976, pp. 36–37 and "Kaiser Steel: The Strategic Question is Whether to Liquidate," *Business Week*, September 8, 1980, pp. 64, 68.

2. See "A Company That's Worth More Dead Than Alive," Peter W. Bernstein, *Fortune*, February 26, 1979, pp. 43–44, quoted with permission.

3. See "Tishman's Newest Design," *Business Week*, July 26, 1976, p. 109 and "Tishman Liquidates a Problem and Itself," *Business Week*, November 7, 1977, pp. 26, 27.

7

Summary and Conclusions

This chapter provides a brief summary of the important aspects of each of the preceding chapters. In Chapter 1, voluntary corporate liquidations were defined as transactions in which all the assets of firms are sold, the proceeds are used to retire existing debt, and remaining funds are distributed to the common stockholders as liquidating dividends. The liquidating firms cease to exist as corporate entities.

This book provides the basis for an assessment of the appropriateness and efficacy of corporate liquidations as a corporate strategic planning tool. The usefulness of corporate liquidations for accomplishing a variety of corporate objectives is illustrated with specific examples in Chapter 2. Chapter 3 discusses various technical aspects of liquidations which must be dealt with by managements undertaking liquidations. Chapter 4 examines the critical role of tax factors in liquidations, while Chapter 5 shows that liquidations are wealth-increasing events for the shareholders of liquidating firms. Although voluntary complete liquidations are an extreme form of disinvestment in that the liquidating firm ceases an independent existence, the liquidation decision is, nonetheless, shown to be rational, well planned, and in the best interests of the common stockholders.

Chapter 2 explores the reasons given by corporate managers for undertaking liquidations. The most frequently cited reason is that the liquidation value of the firm exceeds the market value of the firm's shares or its going concern value. Oftentimes, the assets of the firms can be sold piecemeal to multiple acquirers for more than the trading value of the firm's shares in the securities market. Accordingly, management can put greater value in the hands of the common stockholders by liquidating the firm. The disparity in liquidation value and market value is typically due to the assets being worth more to the buyer than to the seller, and, therefore, the buyer is willing to pay a premium for the assets.

Among the causative factors underlying corporate liquidations discussed in Chapter 2 are: (1) tax factors, (2) regulatory factors, (3) market factors, (4) competition, (5) cessation of business, and (6) government intervention. Each of these factors is illustrated with several specific examples, which are included to describe the variety of situations in which liquidations are useful. Prior to the Tax Reform Act of 1986, a major stimulus to voluntary corporate liquidations was favorable tax treatment on gains from the sale of corporate assets under Section 337 of the Internal Revenue Code of 1954. Specifically, Section 337 stipulated that any gain on the sale of a company's assets is nontaxable to the company provided that the company adopts a plan of complete liquidation prior to the sale of its assets and that thereafter all of the company's assets, except assets retained to meet claims against the company, are fully distributed to shareholders within one year after adoption of the plan. An example was the case of UV Industries, described in Chapter 6. UV Industries avoided a tax liability of $42 million by resorting to this tax provision. However, the Tax Reform Act of 1986 eliminated this tax advantage by requiring that the sale of the liquidating firm's assets be viewed as a taxable transaction to the firm. The likely effects of this change in tax laws will be the discouragement of future liquidations motivated mainly by tax factors, incentive for liquidating firms to restructure their business organizations (e.g., through limited partnerships), a requirement for liquidating firms to demand a higher premium for their assets, and the creation of more important motives for liquidation.

Chapter 2 also identifies the pivotal role of corporate insiders in the liquidation decision. Corporate insiders were defined as officers, directors, and owners of significant amounts of the common stock of liquidating firms. Reaching consensus by the board of directors for the liquidation decision is greatly facilitated by the existence of corporate insiders. An empirical study that was reviewed in Chapter 5 found a significant relationship between the fraction of shares held by corporate insiders and the increase in shareholder wealth associated with the liquidation announcement. One explanation is that in liquidation insiders realize a larger dollar in the wealth because they own a larger fraction of the firm's outstanding shares. Accordingly, they have a greater incentive to search for a buyer willing to pay a premium for the firm's assets.

Chapter 3 describes the mechanical aspects of corporate liquidations. Various topics including the plan of liquidation, which is a part of every liquidation, the proxy statement, and liquidating trust agreement are described. Typically a majority vote of the shareholders is required to approve the plan of liquidation and sale of the firm's assets. If all the assets of the firm are not sold in a twelve-month period following the adoption of the plan of liquidation, the remaining assets are typically transferred to a liquidating trust which is formed by the firm's board of directors for the benefit of the stockholders. The objectives of the liquidating trust are to sell the assets it acquired and distribute the proceeds to the shareholders net of debt payments. Information is provided on employment arrangements for the liquidating firm's employees, treatment of unexercised stock options, and the use of legal, accounting, and other experts in the liquidation process. The chapter also tells how to obtain documents from the Securities and Exchange Commission concerning liquidations of other corporations that may be of interest to executives planning a liquidation.

Major tax aspects of corporate liquidations are covered in Chapter 4. Although, as previously mentioned, the Tax Reform Act of 1986 requires gain or loss recognition on the sale of corporate assets in complete liquidation, there are exceptions to this general rule. Exceptions include the liquidation of controlled subsidiaries and tax-free reorganizations and distributions. While the Tax Reform Act of 1986 requires that gain is recognized by the corporation upon the liquidating distribution or sale of its assets unless an exception applies, an individual shareholder will report gain or loss based upon the difference between the sales proceeds and his tax basis in his stock. In other words, liquidating distributions are taxable to stockholders. Filing requirements for the liquidating firm are presented.

Chapter 5 examines the economic consequences of corporate liquidations. It is assumed that managements would not undertake voluntary liquidations unless they expected them to increase shareholder wealth. Hence, the main focus of the chapter is to ascertain whether these expected increases in shareholder wealth occurred. Three empirical studies were examined in detail. Each of these studies found that voluntary corporate liquidations increased the wealth of shareholders in the liquidating firms. On the buyers' side, one of these studies found that stockholders of the acquiring firms neither gain nor lose, suggesting that the market for corporate acquisitions is highly competitive on the buyers' side.

Three case studies of corporate liquidations are presented in Chapter 6. The particular liquidations examined were selected because they illustrate a wide variety of situations that lead to corporate liquidations. In addition, it was necessary to choose liquidations for which sufficient publicly accessible information was available. The main focus of these case studies was on why these firms decided to liquidate.

The first case study in Chapter 6 was concerned with Kaiser Industries Corporation (KIC). KIC was a holding company whose principal assets were controlling interests in Kaiser Steel Corporation, Kaiser Aluminum and Chemical, and Kaiser Cement and Gypsum. The board of directors of KIC decided to liquidate the firm primarily because KIC's common stockholders would have greater equity security value than if they continued to own the firm's common stock. The reason is that prior to the liquidation, KIC's common stock historically traded at a substantial discount from the combined market value of its common stockholdings in Kaiser Steel, Kaiser Aluminum and Chemical, and Kaiser Cement and Gypsum. By liquidating KIC, the firm's stockholders would have direct ownership of these three stocks, and the basis for the historical discount would be eliminated. The reason that the discount existed was the poor performance of Kaiser Steel. KIC had attempted to sell or merge Kaiser Steel, but there were no willing buyers. Accordingly, complete liquidation was viewed as expedient.

Unlike Kaiser Industries Corporation, UV Industries' liquidation was precipitated by a very lucrative outside offer to purchase UV's largest and most profitable asset. Reliance Electric offered $345 million to purchase Federal Pacific Electric Company, a wholly owned subsidiary of UV Industries. UV's management was concerned that the stock market consistently undervalued UV's assets. However, the offer to purchase Federal Pacific caused UV's stock price to jump significantly. Since Federal Pacific was UV's principal asset and its sale left UV with a huge capital gain and a tax liability of $42 million, UV's board of directors decided to liquidate the entire firm under Section 337 of the Internal Revenue Code so that this tax could be avoided. The liquidation decision also avoided a potential hostile takeover by a corporate raider.

The liquidation of Tishman Realty and Construction Company, Inc., one of the largest publicly held real estate companies, was motivated by management's concern that the company's stock was undervalued in the securities market because of accounting rules that required assets to be carried on the books at historic cost minus depreciation even though the firm's real estate properties had appreciated substantially and generated a large cash flow. By liquidating, shareholders would receive greater benefit from the sale of the company's assets than they would if the company continued in existence. Any assets that the firm could not sell in a twelve-month period following the adoption of the plan of liquidation would be transferred to a limited partnership. The limited partnership has several tax advantages that were not available in the corporate form of organization.

APPENDIXES

Notice of Special Meeting of Shareholders: House of Ronnie, Inc.

HOUSE OF RONNIE, INC.
ONE PENNSYLVANIA PLAZA
NEW YORK, NEW YORK 10001

NOTICE OF SPECIAL MEETING OF SHAREHOLDERS
AUGUST 11, 1981

To The Shareholders:

NOTICE IS HEREBY GIVEN that a Special Meeting of Shareholders of House of Ronnie, Inc., a New York corporation (the "Company"), has been called for and will be held at 10:00 A.M., Eastern Daylight Saving Time, on Tuesday, August 11, 1981 at Marriott's Essex House, 160 Central Park South, New York, New York, for the following purposes:

1. To consider and vote upon a proposed to sell all of the assets and business of the Company to CM-Ronnie Holdings, Inc., pursuant to an Agreement for Purchase and Sale of Assets, and subsequently liquidate and dissolve the Company in conformity with Section 337 of the Internal Revenue Code of 1954, as amended, and Article 10 of the New York Business Corporation Law.

2. To authorize an amendment to the Certificate of Incorporation of the Company to change its corporate name to "Harvjack Corp."; and

3. To transact such other business as may properly come before the meeting or any adjournment or adjournments thereof.

The Board of Directors has fixed the close of business on June 29, 1981 as the record date for the determination of the shareholders entitled to notice of, and to vote at, the meeting or any adjournment or adjournments thereof. The list of shareholders entitled to vote at the meeting will be available for the examination of any shareholder at the Company's principal executive offices at One Pennsylvania Plaza, New York, New York 10001, for ten days prior to the meeting.

WHETHER OR NOT YOU EXPECT TO ATTEND THE MEETING, PLEASE FILL IN, SIGN, AND DATE THE ACCOMPANYING PROXY AND RETURN IT IN THE ENCLOSED STAMPED ENVELOPE. THE GIVING OF SUCH PROXY WILL NOT AFFECT YOUR RIGHT TO REVOKE SUCH PROXY OR TO VOTE IN PERSON SHOULD YOU LATER DECIDE TO ATTEND THE MEETING. THE AFFIRMATIVE VOTE OF AT LEAST TWO-THIRDS OF ALL OUTSTANDING SHARES OF THE COMPANY IS REQUIRED TO CARRY THE PROPOSAL TO APPROVE THE SALE. THE RIGHT OF SHAREHOLDERS TO DISSENT IS SET FORTH IN THE PROXY STATEMENT AND FURTHER DESCRIBED IN EXHIBIT D ANNEXED THERETO.

By Order of the Board of Directors

LOUIS SCHACHTER
Secretary

New York, New York
July 20, 1981

THIS TRANSACTION HAS NOT BEEN APPROVED OR DISAPPROVED BY THE SECURITIES AND EXCHANGE COMMISSION NOR HAS THE COMMISSION PASSED UPON THE FAIRNESS OR MERITS OF SUCH TRANSACTION NOR UPON THE ACCURACY OR ADEQUACY OF THE INFORMATION CONTAINED IN THIS DOCUMENT. ANY REPRESENTATION TO THE CONTRARY IS UNLAWFUL.

TABLE OF CONTENTS

APPENDIX B

Summary of Proposed Plan of Liquidation and Dissolution: Bates Manufacturing Company, Inc.

BATES MANUFACTURING COMPANY, INCORPORATED
850 THIRD AVENUE
NEW YORK, NEW YORK 10022

PROXY STATEMENT
FOR SPECIAL MEETING TO BE HELD MAY 24, 1979

THE PROPOSED LIQUIDATION HAS NOT BEEN APPROVED OR DISAPPROVED BY THE SECURITIES AND EXCHANGE COMMISSION NOR HAS THE COMMISSION PASSED UPON THE ACCURACY OR ADEQUACY OF THESE PROXY MATERIALS.

SUMMARY OF CERTAIN HIGHLIGHTS

The following is a summary, for the convenience of stockholders, of certain information with regard to matters to be considered at the Special Meeting. The summary is necessarily incomplete and selective, and stockholders should carefully read the more detailed sections of the Proxy Statement, and particularly, the specific sections referred to in this summary:

GENERAL INFORMATION

Company Soliciting Proxies
(page 9)

Bates Manufacturing Company, Incorporated, a Delaware corporation ("Bates").

Date, Time and Place of Special Meeting
(page 9)

May 24, 1979, 11.00 a.m., local time, at the Hotel Roanoke, 19 Jefferson Street, N.W., Roanoke, Virginia 24011.

Record Date
(page 11)

Only holders of record of Bates Common Stock at the close of business on April 6, 1979, are entitled to vote at the Special Meeting.

Purpose of Meeting
(page 9)

(1) To consider and act upon a proposal for the adoption of a Plan of Complete Liquidation and Dissolution of Bates (the "Plan"), attached as Annex I to the Proxy Statement, which will constitute approval of an Amended and Restated Agreement, dated as of January 17, 1979, as amended and restated as of February 21, 1979 (the "Agreement"), among Bates and its subsidiary, Virginia Iron, Coal and Coke Company ("VICC"), and American Natural Resources Company ("ANR"), and its subsidiaries, ANR Coal Company ("ANR Coal") and VICC Land Company ("VICC Land"), and a related Escrow Agreement to be entered into among such parties with Citibank, N.A. at the closing of the transaction. (See "Proposed ANR Transaction and Plan of Complete Liquidation and Dissolution".) A copy of the Agreement and the Escrow Agreement are attached as Annex II to the Proxy Statement. See "Terms of Agreement and Escrow Agreement" below.

(2) To consider and act upon a proposal to amend the Certificate of Incorporation of Bates to change the corporate name of Bates to "BAV Liquidating Corporation".

(3) To transact such other business as may properly come before the meeting.

Required Vote of Outstanding Shares (page 11)	Under Delaware law each of the proposals requires the favorable vote of the holders of a majority of the outstanding shares of Common Stock of Bates. On April 6, 1979, there were issued and outstanding 1,651,423 shares of Bates Common Stock.
Principal Stockholders . . . . . . (page 12)	Vicoal, Inc., a New York corporation ("Vicoal"), presently owns 484,027 shares of Bates Common Stock, and certain of Vicoal's stockholders (including Lawrence I. Schneider, Chairman of the Board of Bates, Philip S. Sassower, President and a Director of Bates, and Adolf Marcus, a Director of Bates) presently own an aggregate of 41,000 shares of Bates Common Stock, representing a total of 31.8% of the issued and outstanding shares of Bates Common Stock. Vicoal has adopted its own plan of liquidation and the shares of Bates Common Stock owned by Vicoal may be distributed to the Vicoal stockholders prior to the Special Meeting. Vicoal and its controlling stockholders have advised Bates that they intend to vote such stock in favor of the adoption of the proposed Plan and the other matters to be considered at the meeting. See "Voting Securities and Principal Stockholders".
Business of Bates . . . . (page 33)	Bates is engaged, through VICC, in the leasing and contracting, to independent operators, of owned coal lands located in Virginia and Kentucky. Bates is also engaged, through its subsidiary, Avery Coal Co. Inc. ("Avery"), in the contracting to independent operators of owned and leased coal lands located in Pennsylvania. Both coal subsidiaries are engaged in selling either as principal or agent through their own sales organizations, the coal produced by others, after storing, processing and loading such coal from their facilities, principally to power companies, exporters, steel producers and industrial users. See "Information Concerning Bates".
Terms of Agreement and Escrow Agreement (page 60)	The Agreement provides for the sale by VICC of its properties, assets and business (the "VICC Assets") to VICC Land for an aggregate cash consideration of $104,524,860, and the assumption of certain liabilities of VICC. In April, 1979, VICC distributed as a dividend to Bates intercompany receivables owing from Bates to VICC and from Avery to VICC in the amount of $19,724,619, so as to eliminate intercompany indebtedness. (See "Proposed ANR Transaction and Plan of Complete Liquidation and Dissolution"). Pursuant to the Escrow Agreement, the amount of $3,000,000 (unless title insurance relating to the real property of VICC is obtained by ANR, in which event such escrow is to be reduced to the amount of $2,000,000) of the cash consideration will be held by Citibank, N.A., as Escrow Agent, to provide security for any loss or expense incurred by ANR or its subsidiaries by reason of a breach of certain of the representations and warranties contained in the Agreement or by the failure of Bates to satisfy certain tax liabilities as therein provided.

Pre-Closing Settlement Agreement with ANR (page 62)

Under a Pre-Closing Settlement Agreement made with ANR in April, 1979, VICC has agreed to pay at the Closing, the amount of $745,000 in considerations for the agreement by ANR, VICC Land and ANR Coal not to make any claim, with respect to the alleged breach of any representation or warranty in the Agreement arising out of certain advances to, and equipment repurchase commitments for the benefit of, independent contract operators of three newly developed mines in Wise County, Virginia, and certain investments in a coal processing plant constructed and operated by an independent processor to process refuse coal piles located at Toms Creek, Virginia. See "Pre-Closing Settlement Agreement with ANR".

Opinion of Investment Banker (page 68)

Goldman, Sachs & Co., New York, New York, has acted as Bates' exclusive financial advisor in connection with the negotiations leading to the Agreement. Goldman, Sachs & Co. has delivered its opinion to the Bates Board of Directors that the financial consideration to be received pursuant to the Agreement is fair to Bates. Goldman, Sachs & Co. will receive for its services in connection with the proposed transaction a fee of $1,300,561, contingent upon closing pursuant to the Agreement.

Pending Litigation . . . . (page 53)

Bates, its former parent, Arcs Equities Corp. ("Arcs") and certain related parties, including persons who are officers and Directors of Bates and Arcs, are defendants in a pending purported class action brought on behalf of persons who sold shares of Arcs and Bates Common Stock. This action alleges certain violations of fiduciary duties and certain violations of the Federal securities laws. Since April, 1978, Bates has advanced a total of $21,992 as fees and expenses to the attorneys who are representing Directors of Bates in the action. Another action brought derivatively on behalf of Bates by a stockholder alleging diversion of a corporate opportunity to purchase shares of Bates Common Stock was settled and dismissed on December 14, 1978, by Order and Judgment of the Supreme Court of the State of New York, County of New York, after notice to stockholders and a hearing. Since January, 1976, Bates paid a total of $61,954 as fees and expenses to the attorneys who represented Directors of Bates who were defendants in such action. Also, as the settlement of the derivative action, Bates paid an aggregate of $70,000 as fees and expenses to the attorneys for the plaintiff and for services of the Referee in the action. Additional information with respect to these actions is set forth under the heading "Litigation."

Bates Common Stock Price Range and
  Dividend Policy
   (page 17)

The price of Bates Common Stock on the New York Stock Exchange ranged during the calendar year 1978, and through March 31, 1979, from a low of $35.50 per share to a high of $65.75 per share. The closing price of Bates Common Stock on the Exchange on April 20, 1979, was $59.875. On October 4, 1978, the last trading day prior to the announcement of the agreement, in principle, by the Bates Board of Directors to the proposed ANR transaction, and the intention to seek stockholder authorization of a plan of complete liquidation and dissolution, the closing price of Bates Common Stock was $65.375 per share. Quarterly cash dividends have been paid on Bates Common Stock since the dividend paid on December 31, 1975, at the rate of $.20 per share per quarter. In the event the Plan is adopted, it is anticipated that no further dividends will be paid. See "Price Range and Dividend Policy" for information concerning market prices of Bates Common Stock and dividends.

ITEM I — THE PLAN

Terms of the Plan
  (page 58)

The Plan contemplates the complete liquidation of Bates and pro rata distribution to its stockholders in one or more liquidating distributions of its assets, including the proceeds from the sale of any assets, after provision for all claims, obligations, including contingent liabilities and expenses, and its dissolution, within a twelve-month period beginning with the date of the Special Meeting. If the Plan is adopted by the stockholders of Bates a separate Plan of Complete Liquidation and Dissolution of VICC (the "VICC Plan") under Section 337 of the Internal Revenue Code will be adopted by VICC on the date of the Special Meeting. The Plan provides for the sale of the VICC Assets pursuant to the Agreement; the distribution of the proceeds of the ANR transaction to Bates in liquidation of VICC; the sale or disposition of Bates' remaining assets, including the sale of Avery or the distribution of the capital stock of Avery ("Avery Stock") to Bates stockholders; the payment or making adequate provision for claims, obligations, including contingent liabilities and expenses; the distribution of all the assets of Bates to the Bates stockholders, and the dissolution of Bates. All distributions are subject to prior determination of the Board of Directors that all claims, obligations, including contingent liabilities and expenses of Bates and the costs and expenses of liquidation, have been paid or adequately provided for.

Dissolution of Bates
  (page 58)

Prior to the end of the twelve-month period, a certificate of dissolution of Bates will be filed with the Secretary of State of Delaware.

Initial Liquidating Distribution
  (page 66)

The Board of Directors has stated its intention to declare an initial pro rata liquidating distribution of $52 per share, or an aggregate of approximately $86,000,000.

Subsequent Distributions
(page 66)

Distributions may be made subsequent to the initial liquidating distribution, at such times and in such manner, whether in cash or in kind, as the Board of Directors may determine. The amounts of subsequent distributions cannot be determined at this time. The Board of Directors will not make a final distribution of the assets of Bates until claims and obligations of Bates, including the obligations under the Agreement and the claims being asserted in the pending litigation, have either been disposed of or adequately provided for. In accordance with the requirements of the Plan, all of the assets of Bates, including any contingent assets, will be distributed to the Bates stockholders within twelve months after the Special Meeting. Some portion of the subsequent distributions may be made to the stockholders by distributing certain assets to trustees in dissolution who will receive and hold all such assets on behalf of the stockholders, subject only to the obligations, claims and expenses. (See "Trustees in Dissolution" below.)

Trustees in Dissolution
(page 66)

If it is determined during the twelve-month period following the adoption of the Plan that at the expiration of such period there may be payments for distributions owing to unlocated stockholders, any contingent or other assets which it is not practicable to distribute directly to the stockholders within the twelve-month period, or if any liabilities of Bates remain unsettled, application may be made under Delaware law prior to the expiration of the twelve-month period, for the appointment of one or more Bates Directors as a trustee or trustees in dissolution on behalf of Bates stockholders. Upon the appointment of the trustee or trustees, all the assets of Bates shall be vested in the trustee or trustees and Bates shall have no further interest in its assets. Prior to the expiration of the twelve-month period, such trustee or trustees will execute a document acknowledging and declaring that the beneficial interest in the assets held by him or them, including any uncollected claims or contingent or other assets or any contingency reserve, belongs to the stockholders of Bates and that the trustee or trustees hold such assets solely for the benefit of the Bates stockholders, subject only to obligations, claims and expenses.

No Appraisal Rights
(page 67)

Under Delaware law, Bates stockholders are not entitled to any rights of appraisal for their shares.

Recommendation of Bates Board of Directors
(page 59)

The Board of Directors of Bates has unanimously approved the Plan and recommends its adoption by the stockholders. See "Reasons for Liquidation".

Reasons for Liquidation
(page 59)

Vicoal, as a principal stockholder of Bates, and the Management of Bates, believe the sale of the VICC Assets pursuant to the Agreement is a favorable opportunity for all Bates stockholders to liquidate their investment in Bates shares. The Board of Directors of Bates believes that the adoption of the Plan and the dissolution of Bates is deemed to be expedient and in the best interest of Bates and its stockholders, particularly in light of new strip mining laws, which have caused a shift from strip mining to deep mining of Bates' coal reserves in Virginia and Kentucky and will necessitate substantially increased capital expenditures. See "Information Concerning Bates". In addition, the Board has considered the opinion of Goldman, Sachs & Co. with respect to the fairness of the financial consideration to be received pursuant to the Agreement. See "Information Concerning Bates" and "Proposed ANR Transaction and Plan of Complete Liquidation and Dissolution".

Federal Tax Consequences
(page 64)

With certain exceptions, no gain or loss will be recognized to Bates or VICC as a result of the sale of the VICC Assets, provided that Bates and VICC distribute all of their cash and other assets (less payments or making adequate provision for claims, obligations, including contingent liabilities and expenses) to their stockholders within twelve months from the adoption of the Plan. Moreover, with certain exceptions, no gain or loss will be recognized by Bates upon the distribution of its assets pursuant to the Plan. Gain or loss will be recognized to each Bates stockholder to the extent of the difference between the amount of cash plus the fair market value of any other assets received by the stockholder or the trustee or trustees in dissolution on his behalf and the adjusted tax basis of such stockholder's shares. Provided the shares of Bates Common Stock are capital assets in the hands of these stockholders, the gain or loss will constitute capital gain or loss. See "Federal Income Tax Consequences".

STOCKHOLDERS ARE ADVISED THAT THE COMPLETE LIQUIDATION OF BATES WILL BE A TAXABLE TRANSACTION TO THEM AND THAT THEY WILL BE REQUIRED TO RECOGNIZE GAIN OR LOSS TO THE EXTENT OF THE DIFFERENCE BETWEEN THEIR TAX BASIS IN THEIR BATES STOCK AND THE CASH OR OTHER ASSETS DISTRIBUTED BY BATES. ANY SUCH GAIN OR LOSS WILL CONSTITUTE CAPITAL GAIN OR LOSS TO THOSE BATES STOCKHOLDERS IN WHOSE HANDS THE BATES COMMON STOCK IS A CAPITAL ASSET. SEE "FEDERAL INCOME TAX CONSEQUENCES".

Reports to Stockholders
(page 71)

During the liquidation Bates presently intends to keep its stockholders apprised of material corporate events through the issuance of press releases, the filing of reports under the Securities Exchange Act of 1934 and the dissemination of stockholders' reports.

Trading of Bates Common Stock
(page 66)

The New York Stock Exchange, Inc. (the "Exchange") has advised Bates that the continued listing status of its Common Stock will be reviewed following the Special Meeting. The Exchange, assuming that the Bates stockholders adopt the Plan, does not presently intend to suspend further dealings immediately or to make application to the Securities and Exchange Commission to delist Bates Common Stock. However, no assurance can be given that Bates Common Stock will continue to be eligible for listing and trading throughout the period covered by the Plan. The Exchange noted that it may, at any time, suspend a security if it believes that further dealings in the security on the Exchange are not advisable. If Bates Common Stock is delisted, it is expected that trading in shares of Bates Common Stock will be continued on the over-the-counter market.

ITEM II — AMENDMENT OF CERTIFICATE OF INCORPORATION

Change of Corporate Name
(page 71)

The Bates Board of Directors proposes to amend the Bates Certificate of Incorporation to change the name of Bates to "BAV Liquidating Corporation". The change is proposed as a result of an agreement entered into by Bates in connection with the sale of a former subsidiary on December 31, 1976, which assigned the rights relating to the name "Bates" to such subsidiary and in which Bates undertook to change its corporate name at its next Annual Meeting of Stockholders. Since no meeting of stockholders was held subsequent to that transaction the matter is being presented to the Special Meeting. If the amendment to the Certificate of Incorporation is approved, existing stock certificates in the name of "Bates" will continue to be valid. No new certificates in the new name of Bates are intended to be issued. See "Proposal to Amend The Certificate of Incorporation".

ITEM III — OTHER MATTERS

The Management is not aware of any other matters which may come before the meeting. However, if any other business should properly come before the meeting, the persons named in the accompanying proxy will vote upon the business in accordance with their best judgment

SELECTED CONSOLIDATED FINANCIAL INFORMATION OF BATES

(Amounts in thousands except per share amounts)

	Year Ended				
	Dec. 28, 1974	Jan. 3, 1976	Jan. 1, 1977	Dec. 31, 1977	Dec. 30, 1978
Statements of Earnings (Loss):					
Net sales and operating revenues	$88,111	$93,393	$68,002	$87,736	$91,880
Earnings of continuing operations	12,135	7,878	3,850	6,889	4,265
Discontinued operations	(1,116)	(63)	(4,524)	(3,826)	(660)
Net earnings (loss) applicable to shares of common stock	10,332	7,815	(674)	3,063	3,605
Net earnings (loss) per share of common stock:					
Primary:					
Continuing operations	8.85	3.81	1.91	3.41	2.35
Discontinued operations	(.86)	(.03)	(2.24)	(1.89)	(.36)
Net	7.99	3.78	(.33)	1.52	1.99
Fully diluted:					
Continuing operations	4.71	3.40	1.91	3.41	2.35
Discontinued operations	(.42)	(.03)	(2.24)	(1.89)	(.36)
Net	4.29	3.37	(.33)	1.52	1.99
Average number of outstanding shares of common stock:					
Primary	1,293	2,024	2,021	2,021	1,816
Fully diluted	2,626	2,316	2,021	2,021	1,816
Balance Sheet (at end of period)					
Total Assets	$71,003	$71,413	$61,090	$60,823	$53,906
Debt, including current portion	9,935	9,028	6,400	2,391	5,750
Stockholders' Equity	45,864	44,902	42,611	44,058	34,790
Cash dividends per share of common stock	.20	.35	.80	.80	.80
Book value per share of common stock					21.07

SELECTED PRO FORMA BALANCE SHEET
INFORMATION WITH RESPECT TO BATES
(Reflecting ANR Transaction)

	December 30, 1978
Total Assets	$129,726,000
Total Liabilities and Deferred Federal Income Taxes	10,958,000
Stockholders' Equity	118,768,000*
Book value per share of Common Stock	$71.92

* Reflects increase of $83,978,000 attributable to the excess of cash received over book value of net assets sold.

APPENDIX C

Plan of Complete Liquidation and Dissolution: Austral Oil Company, Inc.

PLAN OF COMPLETE LIQUIDATION AND DISSOLUTION OF AUSTRAL OIL COMPANY INCORPORATED

(A Delaware Corporation)

This Plan of Complete Liquidation and Dissolution (the "Plan") is for the purpose of effecting the complete, voluntary liquidation and dissolution of Austral Oil Company Incorporated, a Delaware corporation (the "Company"), in accordance with and pursuant to the provisions of Section 337 of the United States Internal Revenue Code of 1954, as amended (the "Code"), and Sections 271, 275, 278 and other applicable sections of the Delaware General Corporation Law, in substantially the following manner:

1.   This Plan shall be effective on the date (the "Effective Date") on which it is adopted by affirmative vote of the holders of a majority of the outstanding shares of common stock, $.25 par value, of the Company ("Common Stock") entitled to vote thereon, voting at a meeting of the holders of Common Stock of the Company (the "Stockholders") called for such purpose.

2.   After the Effective Date, the Company shall cease to carry on any business except and insofar as necessary for the sale of its assets and for the proper winding up of the Company pursuant to Section 278 of the Delaware General Corporation Law, including, without limitation, the performance of the Company's obligations under the Agreement for Sale of Properties by and between the Company and The Superior Oil Company (the "Agreement") and the distribution to a Liquidating Trust of the remaining assets not sold under the Agreement or otherwise and not practicably distributable in kind directly to Stockholders. The Company shall have continuing authority to sell, lease, exchange or otherwise convert to cash all or any part of its assets in accordance with the terms and provisions of this Plan, and to make such arrangements with respect to employee compensation as may be advisable, including without limitation arranging for payment of compensation in connection with the surrender or cancellation of any options outstanding under the Company's two qualified stock option plans.

3.   As promptly as is practicable after the Effective Date, the Company shall (a) take the necessary steps to complete formal dissolution under the Delaware General Corporation Law, (b) withdraw from all jurisdictions in which it is qualified to do business, (c) collect or make provisions for the collection of all accounts receivable, debts and claims owing to the Company, and (d) pay and discharge or make adequate provision for the payment and discharge of all the liabilities, debts, claims, expenses and obligations of the Company.

4.   The Company shall close its stock transfer books at the close of business on the record date fixed by the Board of Directors (the "Directors") for the first liquidating distribution (the "Record Date") and thereafter certificates representing Common Stock shall not be assignable or transferable on the books of the Company except by will, intestate succession or operation of law.

5.   The Company shall distribute, as expeditiously as reasonably practicable, in cash or in kind its assets remaining after sales, exchanges, leases and other conversions to cash and after payment or provision for payment of claims, obligations, liabilities, debts and expenses, pro rata, to the Stockholders on the Record Date in one or more distributions in complete liquidation of the Company. Without further Stockholder action, liquidating distributions shall be made in such amount, upon such dates and in such manner, consistent with the provisions of this Plan, as the Directors may determine. Any partial distribution shall be one of a series of two or more distributions in complete liquidation of the Company; provided, however, that all distributions made by the Company, including assets distributed to trusts as set forth below, shall be made within a twelve-month period beginning on the Effective Date. The Stockholders shall surrender their stock certificates

(or furnish indemnity bonds in case of lost or destroyed certificates) as a condition to their receipt of the initial distribution.

6. Prior to the expiration of the twelve-month period beginning on the Effective Date, a petition shall be filed with the Delaware Court of Chancery for the appointment of a trustee of a Missing Stockholders Trust' to which there will be transferred (i) liquidating distributions distributable to Stockholders who have not surrendered their stock certificates (or furnished indemnity bonds in case of lost or destroyed certificates), and (ii) cash payable to those Stockholders who have not cashed checks previously issued in payment of liquidating distributions. The amounts so transferred shall be held by such trustee on behalf of such Stockholders and for their benefit and shall be disposed of pursuant to the provisions of orders of the Delaware Court of Chancery and applicable forfeiture or escheat laws. From and after the date of the appointment of such trustee and the Company's transfer of funds, assets and properties thereto, the Company shall have no interest of any character in and to any such funds, assets or properties and thereafter all of such funds, assets and properties shall be held solely for the benefit of the Stockholders entitled thereto.

7. Prior to the expiration of the twelve-month period beginning on the Effective Date, a petition shall be filed with the Delaware Court of Chancery for the appointment of a trustee of a Liquidating Trust (the "Trustee") for the benefit of the Stockholders to which there will be transferred all of the right, title and interest of the Company in and to all of the funds, assets and properties of the Company of every kind and character not theretofore distributed (with the exception of an amount of cash deemed necessary to satisfy debts, claims, obligations, liabilities and expenses of the Company including contingent debts, claims, obligations, liabilities and expenses, if any, that the Company determines should not be paid by the Liquidating Trust) and the Trustee shall be authorized:

(a) to collect, liquidate, or otherwise convert into cash, all receivables, debts, claims and assets of the Company,

(b) to pay, discharge or make adequate provision for the payment and discharge of all debts, claims, obligations, liabilities and expenses of the Company that are to be paid by the Trust, with the right to prosecute and defend litigation (in the name of the Company or otherwise), and

(c) to distribute to the Stockholders all the net proceeds remaining in the hands of such Trustee as soon as it is practicable to do so.

From and after the date of the appointment of such Trustee and the Company's transfer of funds, assets and properties thereto, the Company shall have no interest of any character in and to any such funds, assets or properties and thereafter all of such funds, assets and properties shall be held solely for the benefit of the Stockholders, subject only to unsatisfied claims, obligations, liabilities, debts, and expenses to be paid by the Trust.

8. Any assets distributable to any creditor of the Company who is unknown or cannot be found, or who is under a disability and for whom there is no legal representative, shall be disposed of pursuant to the provisions of orders of the Delaware Court of Chancery and applicable forfeiture or escheat laws.

9. All sales, payments, provisions, transfers, distributions and liquidations or other actions to be performed by the Company hereunder shall be accomplished within a twelve-month period beginning on the Effective Date (with the possible exception of settlement of debts, claims, obligations, liabilities and expenses pursuant to Section 278 of the Delaware General Corporation Law), including actions taken in connection with assets distributed to the Trustee. The appropriate

officers of the Company are authorized and directed (a) as promptly as practicable after the Effective Date, to execute, acknowledge and file the certificate required by Section 275 of the Delaware General Corporation Law, (b) within thirty (30) days after the Effective Date, to execute and file a United States Treasury Form 966 pursuant to Section 6043 of the Code and such additional forms and reports with the Internal Revenue Service as may be appropriate in connection with this Plan and the carrying out thereof, and (c) to perform all acts which are deemed necessary or advisable to wind up the affairs of the Company and dissolve.

10.   Adoption of the Plan by the Stockholders shall constitute full and complete authority to the proper officers of the Company, without further Director or Stockholder action (except for any further Stockholder or Director approval required by law), to do and perform any and all acts and to make, execute and deliver any and all agreements, conveyances, assignments, transfers, certificates and other documents of every kind and character which such officers deem necessary or appropriate to carry out the provisions of the Plan.

APPENDIX D

Agreement for Sale of Properties by and between Austral Oil Company, Inc., and The Superior Oil Company

Agreement for Sale of Properties

BY AND BETWEEN

AUSTRAL OIL COMPANY INCORPORATED

AND

THE SUPERIOR OIL COMPANY

AGREEMENT FOR SALE OF PROPERTIES
TABLE OF CONTENTS

TABLE OF EXHIBITS

TABLE OF DEFINITIONS

AGREEMENT FOR SALE OF PROPERTIES

This Agreement for Sale of Properties ("Agreement") made and entered into as of the 10th day of March, 1978, by and between Austral Oil Company Incorporated, a Delaware corporation ("Austral"), and The Superior Oil Company, a Nevada corporation ("Superior"),

WITNESSETH:

WHEREAS, Austral desires to sell and convey to Superior and Superior desires to purchase and acquire from Austral the Properties, as herein defined, all upon the terms and conditions set forth herein;

NOW, THEREFORE, in consideration of the mutual agreements contained herein and the payments, conveyances and assignments herein provided for, Austral and Superior agree as follows:

1. **SALE AND PURCHASE OF THE PROPERTIES.** Subject to the conditions and upon the terms and for the consideration hereinafter set forth, Austral agrees to grant, bargain, sell and convey to Superior, and Superior agrees to purchase and acquire from Austral the following described properties and assets owned by Austral, whether directly or indirectly, legally or beneficially, except to the extent that they may constitute Excluded Interests, as herein defined (the "Properties"), all as such exist 7:00 a.m. on the Closing Date, as herein defined:

1.1 *Domestic Properties.*

1.1.1 All properties from which crude oil, natural gas, casinghead gas, drip gasoline, natural gasoline, petroleum, natural gas liquids, condensate, products, liquids and other hydrocarbons and other minerals or materials of every kind and description (the "Substances") are or may be produced or recovered, or which relate to the ownership or production of Substances, whether such properties are in the nature of fee interests, leasehold interests, working interests, royalty, overriding royalty or other non-working or carried interests, operating rights or other mineral rights of every nature relating to the ownership or production of Substances (the "Oil and Gas Properties").

1.1.2 All oil, condensate or natural gas wells, water source wells, and water and other types of injection wells, whether producing, operating, shut-in or temporarily abandoned and all equipment used or held for use in connection with the production of Substances from the Oil and Gas Properties and all severed Substances (except Substances produced and sold prior to the Closing Date by or for the account of Austral) produced from the Oil and Gas Properties.

1.1.3 All physical facilities or interests therein, including but not limited to tanks and tank batteries, gas plants, disposal facilities, buildings, structures, field separators and liquid extractors, compressors, pumps, pumping units, valves, fittings, machinery and parts, engines, boilers, meters, apparatus, implements, tools, appliances, cables, wires, towers, casing, tubing and rods, gathering lines or other pipelines, field gathering systems, field offices and the furniture and fixtures contained therein, trucks, tractors, boats, and all other fixtures and equipment of every type and description to the extent that the same are used or held for use in connection with the ownership or operation of the properties described in Sections 1.1.1 and 1.1.2.

1.1.4 All lands, tenements, hereditaments, appurtenances, surface leases, easements, permits, licenses, servitudes and rights of way in any way appertaining, belonging, affixed or incidental to or used or held for use in connection with the ownership or operation of the properties described in Sections 1.1.1 through 1.1.3.

1.1.5 All leases, options, rights of refusal, contracts, operating agreements or other agreements and instruments to the extent that the same relate, appertain, belong, or are incidental to the properties described in Sections 1.1.1 through 1.1.4.

The properties, interests and agreements referred to in Sections 1.1.1, 1.1.2, 1.1.3, 1.1.4 and 1.1.5 (the "Domestic Properties"), including any liens, charges or encumbrances thereon known to Austral (Superior recognizing that Austral has made no title investigation with respect to certain properties referred to in Section 5.3) are described in Exhibit 1.1 or Exhibit 1.3 except as otherwise noted therein. The liens, charges and encumbrances specified on Exhibit 1.1 or Exhibit 1.3 are herein called the "Permitted Encumbrances".

1.2   *Austral Petroleum Gas Corporation.* 1,000 shares of Common Stock, par value $1.00 per share (the "APG Stock"), of Austral Petroleum Gas Corporation, a Delaware corporation ("APG"), being all the issued and outstanding shares of capital stock of APG, and all inter-company accounts owed by APG to Austral.

1.3   *Contractual Rights with Respect to Certain Property Interests.* Austral's contractual rights and arrangements (including any privileges or liens resulting therefrom) in acting as operating agent for, or participant with, certain co-owners with respect to interests in oil and gas properties acquired by such co-owners through participation in annual or continuing general programs sponsored by Austral or its subsidiaries from 1954 through 1969. The contracts and agreements giving rise to such contractual rights and arrangements, as they exist on the date hereof, are set forth in Exhibit 1.3.

1.4   *Records.* All of Austral's lease files, land files, well files, abstracts, title opinions, accounting records, seismic records and surveys, gravity maps, electric logs, geological and geophysical prospect maps, geological base maps, and other geological or geophysical data and records and other documents and records of every kind and description which relate to the Properties described in Sections 1.1, 1.2 and 1.3 (the "Transferred Records"), including file cabinets or other containers adequate to store the Transferred Records; provided, however, that Austral may with Superior's consent make and retain for its own use or disposition one or more copies of any Transferred Record.

1.5   *Excluded Interests.* Notwithstanding any provision herein to the contrary, excluded from the Properties are the properties, assets, rights and interests of Austral described in Exhibit 1.5 (the "Excluded Interests").

2.   ASSUMPTION OF CERTAIN OBLIGATIONS. Subject to the conditions and upon the terms and for the consideration set forth in this Agreement, Superior agrees to assume, effective as of 7:00 a.m. on the Closing Date, and will pay and discharge the following:

2.1   *Obligations After Closing.* All obligations of Austral to be performed after 7:00 a.m. on the Closing Date under the terms of the leases, contracts, instruments and agreements described on Exhibits 1.1, 1.3 or 5.12, as such Exhibits may be amended and supplemented through and as of the Closing Date; provided, however, that Superior shall not assume the obligation to pay and discharge any refunds including interest and penalties, if any, which may be imposed by the Department of Energy or any component thereof (including the Federal Energy Regulatory Commission) and the Federal Energy Administration and any predecessor governmental agency arising from the sale of Substances from the Domestic Properties other than as expressly provided for in Section 2.2.

2.2   *Certain Refund Obligations.* Liabilities of Austral with respect to which and only to the extent that Superior has received moneys from Austral pursuant to Section 6.2, and liabilities of Austral with respect to refunds including interest and penalties, if any, which may be imposed by (i) the Department of Energy or any component thereof (including the Federal Energy Regulatory Commission) and the Federal Energy Administration and any predecessor governmental agency arising from the sale of Substances produced from the Dean Unit in the Ackerly Field, Dawson County, Texas or (ii) any governmental authority with respect to sales of Substances occurring after September 30, 1977.

2.3   *Royalty and Other Payments.* Liabilities of Austral with respect to which and only to the extent that Superior has received moneys from Austral pursuant to Section 6.3.

2.4 *Certain Income Tax Liabilities.* The obligation to pay to Austral an amount equal to the lesser of (i) the aggregate amount of federal and state income taxes paid by Austral for each calendar year which includes a portion of the Adjustment Period, as herein defined, less the portion, if any, of such tax which equals 48%, or the minimum applicable statutory rate if less than 48%, (plus the applicable state income tax rates) of the net income from investment of funds received from Superior hereunder or (ii) the amount of such taxes paid which equals 48%, or the minimum applicable statutory rate if less than 48%, (plus the applicable state income tax rates) of taxable income of Austral and APG on a consolidated basis derived from operations of the Domestic Properties and APG during the Adjustment Period.

3. PURCHASE PRICE.

3.1 *Method of Computing Purchase Price.* The Purchase Price for the Properties (the "Purchase Price") shall consist of $170,082,922 (being $164,316,000 plus $5,766,922 representing the net current assets and certain other accounts of APG at September 30, 1977) less the Title Adjustment, as herein defined (the "Basic Price"), as such price is adjusted on a dollar for dollar basis from October 1, 1977 to the Closing Date (such period of time being herein referred to as the "Adjustment Period") as follows:

3.1.1. The Basic Price will be increased as follows:

(i) By an amount equal to the interest at the prime rate as established from time to time by First City National Bank of Houston on $164,316,000 from December 15, 1977 to the Closing Date;

(ii) By an amount equal to all costs (other than general and administrative expenses relating to Austral's offices in Houston, Texas) which are incurred and paid by Austral for its own account after September 30, 1977 and which are attributable to the Domestic Properties after such date, but excluding any fines or penalties by local, state or federal governmental agencies (except those assumed by Superior pursuant to Section 2.2) and any costs and expenses arising from or related to any of the transactions contemplated by this Agreement or the other instruments delivered in connection with this Agreement;

(iii) By an amount equal to $6,000 per calendar day during the Adjustment Period (such amount to be in lieu of any general and administrative expenses relating to Austral's offices in Houston, Texas);

(iv) By an amount equal to all advances made by Austral to APG after September 30, 1977; and

(v) By an amount equal to that part of (a) all ad valorem taxes, delay rentals, renewal bonuses with respect to leases which would have otherwise expired after October 1, 1977, and rentals, which were paid by Austral before October 1, 1977 and which are attributable to the Properties after September 30, 1977, and (b) all unearned insurance and bond premiums which were paid by Austral before October 1, 1977 and which are attributable to the Properties (including the assets, business and operations of APG) during the Adjustment Period.

3.1.2 The Basic Price will be decreased as follows:

(i) By an amount equal to the proceeds received by Austral from sales during the Adjustment Period of Substances produced and saved during the Adjustment Period from the Domestic Properties by or for the account of Austral; provided, however, no decrease will be made in the Basic Price arising from the sale of Substances pursuant to that certain Agreement of Purchase and Sale of Liquid Hydrocarbons dated as of June 2, 1977 between Austral and Wanda Petroleum Company (the "Advance Sale Agreement");

(ii)   By an amount equal to all other amounts received by Austral after September 30, 1977 attributable to the Domestic Properties after such date, including but not limited to dry hole, bottom hole and other contributions. and any other proceeds, contributions, refunds, rebates, repayments or receipts of any type or description which are attributable to the Domestic Properties after such date; and

(iii)   By an amount equal to any repayments by APG after September 30, 1977, of intercompany accounts owed by APG to Austral.

3.2   *Procedure for Computing Purchase Price.* After the Closing Date Austral shall prepare a statement of Purchase Price ("Closing Statement") setting forth each adjustment to the Basic Price resulting in the computation of the Purchase Price as set forth in Section 3.1 above. Such Closing Statement shall be prepared in accordance with generally accepted accounting principles and shall be reviewed by Austral's independent accountants. As soon as practicable but no later than 90 days after the Closing Date, Austral shall deliver to Superior the Closing Statement for review by Superior and its independent accountants. which review will include access to the records of Austral and APG pertaining to the Closing Statement and access by Superior's independent accountants to the working papers of Austral's independent accountants pertaining to such statement. Within 15 days from the receipt of the Closing Statement Superior will deliver to Austral a report containing any suggested changes. In the event that Austral and Superior do not agree upon the Closing Statement, the firm of Arthur Young & Company, independent public accountants, is designated to act as an arbitrator and to decide all points of disagreement with respect to the Closing Statement. such decision to be binding upon both parties. The Purchase Price as set forth in the Closing Statement, adjusted to reflect any changes agreed to by Austral and Superior and any changes made by the arbitrator, will be the Purchase Price for purposes of this Agreement. The charges of the arbitrator shall be shared equally by Austral and Superior.

4.   TITLE REQUIREMENTS.

4.1   *Title Opinions and Abstracts.* Austral shall assist Superior in obtaining abstracts of title and title opinions and other title information covering each of the real property interests designated by Superior as "material" on Exhibit 1.1 (the "Material Properties"). Austral shall give Superior access to all lease files. abstracts, supplemental title material and other records relating to the Material Properties that Austral has in its possession.

4.2   *Examination of Title.* Superior shall have the material obtained by it pursuant to Section 4.1 examined and shall obtain such supplemental title material as Superior deems necessary and shall then cause a title opinion to be prepared with respect to each of the Material Properties, and shall submit copies thereof to Austral promptly after their completion. Austral shall bear all reasonable costs and expenses, up to a maximum of $175,000, associated with the expenses of (i) examining title by attorneys who are not officers or regular employees of Superior, and (ii) obtaining any additional abstracts. supplemental abstracts and other supplemental title material and all curative work. If such costs and expenses in the aggregate exceed $175,000, the excess shall be borne by Superior.

4.3   *Cure of Defects.* Counsel for Superior shall examine the title opinions delivered pursuant to Section 4.2 in order to determine whether such opinions confirm that (i) in the case of each interest in a Material Property shown to be owned of record by Austral on Exhibit 1.1, Austral has title to such interest free and clear of all liens, claims or encumbrances except Permitted Encumbrances, and has the right to sell and convey such interest to Superior without the release, consent or waiver of third parties holding preferential purchase rights or rights to consent to the assignment thereof (other than rights to consent by, required notices to, filings with or other actions by governmental entities in connection with the sale or conveyance of federal, state, Indian or other governmental oil and gas leases or interests therein or related thereto, such with respect to any Domestic Property being herein referred to as "Governmental Consents"); (ii) in the case of each interest in a Material Property shown to be owned of record by Oil Participations Incorporated, a Delaware corporation ("OPI"), on Exhibit 1.1, OPI has record title to such interest, and Austral has beneficial interests therein, in each case free and clear of all liens, claims or encumbrances except Permitted Encumbrances, sufficient to result in Austral having the interests shown in Exhibit 1.1 (a) in each unit or well (as the case may be) in which any portion of such Material Property is included and (b) in Material Properties which are not Title Properties, and that Austral has the right to sell and convey such interests to Superior without the release, consent or waiver of third parties holding preferential purchase rights or rights to consent, other than Governmental Consents, to the assignment thereof; and (iii) Exhibit 1.1 accurately reflects Austral's interests (derived from its record or beneficial ownership of interests in each Material Property), and all liens, charges and encumbrances thereon, in each unit or well (as the case may be) in which any portion of a Material Property is included. If any such opinions do not confirm the foregoing, Austral shall use its best efforts to cure all such deficiencies in title set forth in such opinions (the "Unpermitted Deficiencies") and to obtain such releases, consents, other than Governmental Consents, or waivers as are called for in such title opinions.

4.4   Adjustment Events.   If at the Closing, as herein defined, (i) releases, consents or waivers with respect to the preferential purchase rights or consents to assignments, other than Governmental Consents, referred to in Section 4.3 have not been obtained, or (ii) any Unpermitted Deficiencies have not been cured or waived by Superior, then none of the rights, titles or interests of Austral in any Material Property so affected and in any other Domestic Property relating solely to such affected Material Property shall be included in the conveyances contemplated by this Agreement and none of Austral's representations, warranties, covenants or agreements herein shall be deemed to have been made with respect to any Material Property and other related Domestic Property not so conveyed.

4.5   Adjustment — Evaluation.   Superior shall inform Austral of the portion of the Basic Price reasonably allocable to each Material Property subject to a preferential purchase right, and such amount shall be deemed to be the value of any such Material Property excluded from the conveyance contemplated by this Agreement because of the exercise of a preferential purchase right with respect thereto. In the event any Material Property is otherwise excluded from the conveyance contemplated by this Agreement in accordance with and pursuant to Section 4.4, the value of such Material Property shall be determined before the Closing by mutual agreement of Austral and Superior (or, if agreement cannot be reached, by the independent petroleum engineering firm having prepared reserve reports for Austral with respect to such Material Property at December 31, 1976) based upon the following factors: (i) the reserves attributable to the affected Material Property; (ii) future revenues from the affected Material Property; (iii) the value of the affected Material Property as a portion of the Properties; (iv) the amount paid by Superior for the Properties as a whole; and (v) any other factors upon which the parties can mutually agree. The charges of the independent petroleum engineering firm for services rendered pursuant to this Section 4.5 shall be shared equally by Austral and Superior.

4.6   Title Adjustment.   The aggregate value of the affected Material Properties determined pursuant to Section 4.5 is herein referred to as the Title Adjustment.

4.7   Failure to Obtain Title Opinion.   If Superior has not obtained a title opinion as provided for in Section 4.2 with respect to any Material Property on or before the Closing, the provisions of Sections 4.1 through 4.6 hereof shall no longer be applicable to such property. Superior shall deliver to Austral at the Closing a list of all Material Properties with respect to which title opinions have not been obtained (the "Specified Material Properties").

5. REPRESENTATIONS AND WARRANTIES BY AUSTRAL. Austral represents and warrants as follows:

5.1 *Organization.*

5.1.1   Austral is a corporation duly organized, validly existing and in good standing under the laws of the State of Delaware and has all requisite corporate power and authority to own the Properties, to conduct its business as presently conducted by it, to enter into this Agreement and to carry out the transactions contemplated hereby. Austral conducts business or owns property in no state or jurisdiction other than the state of its incorporation and the jurisdictions listed on Exhibit 5.1.1. Austral is qualified to do business as a foreign corporation and is in good standing in each of such states or jurisdictions, except as otherwise disclosed on Exhibit 5.1.1.

5.1.2   APG is a wholly-owned subsidiary of Austral, is a corporation duly organized, validly existing and in good standing under the laws of the State of Delaware, has all requisite corporate power and authority to own its properties and to conduct its business as presently being conducted by it, and conducts business or owns property in no state or jurisdiction other than the state of its incorporation and Texas, being the only state or jurisdiction in which it is required to be qualified to do business as a foreign corporation. APG is qualified to do business as a foreign corporation and is in good standing in Texas.

5.1.3   OPI is a wholly-owned subsidiary of the University of Texas Ex-Students' Association, is duly organized, validly existing and in good standing under the laws of the State of Delaware, has all requisite corporate power and authority to own its properties and to conduct its business as presently being conducted by it, and conducts business or owns property in no states or jurisdictions other than the state of its incorporation and the states and jurisdictions listed on Exhibit 5.1.3. OPI is qualified to do business as a foreign corporation and is in good standing in each of such states or jurisdictions except as otherwise disclosed in Exhibit 5.1.3. OPI engages in no business other than holding record title to certain properties owned beneficially by Austral and the co-owners referred to in Section 1.3 and acting on behalf of Austral and the co-owners with respect thereto.

5.1.4   Austral has delivered to Superior true and correct copies of the Certificates of Incorporation and by-laws of Austral, APG and OPI, as amended to date.

5.2 *Ownership of Stock.*

5.2.1   The APG Stock has been duly authorized, validly issued and is fully paid and nonassessable. The APG Stock is all of the authorized, issued and outstanding capital stock of APG. Austral owns all of the APG Stock and on the Closing Date the APG Stock will be free and clear of all liens, claims, charges or encumbrances, except as set forth on Exhibit 5.2.1 (the lien described on such Exhibit on the date hereof is herein referred to as the "Pledge"). No options, conversion or other rights, agreements or commitments of any kind obligating APG to issue any shares of capital stock or any securities convertible into or exchangeable for any such shares, are outstanding and no authorization therefor has been given.

5.2.2   The outstanding capital stock of OPI (the "OPI Stock") consists of 1,000 shares of $1.00 par value common stock, all of which has been duly authorized, validly issued and is fully paid and nonassessable. The OPI Stock is all of the authorized, issued and outstanding capital stock of OPI. The University of Texas Ex-Students' Association, a Texas non-profit corporation, owns all of the OPI Stock free and clear of all liens, claims, charges or encumbrances except for a preferential right of purchase in Austral which will be assigned by Austral to Superior at the Closing. No options, conversion or other rights, agreements or commitments of any kind obligating OPI to issue any shares of capital stock or any securities convertible into or exchangeable for any such shares, are outstanding and no authorization therefor has been given.

5.3 *Certain Properties.* Exhibit 1.1 accurately reflects the information required to be shown thereon. Austral has good and indefeasible title to Austral's interests as shown on Exhibit 1.1 in the Oil and Gas Properties designated on Exhibit 1.1 as Title Properties (the "Title Properties") which are owned of record by Austral, free and clear of all liens, claims or encumbrances except Permitted Encumbrances. OPI has good and indefeasible title to interests in each Title Property which is owned of record by OPI and Austral has beneficial interests therein, in each case free and clear of all liens, claims or encumbrances except Permitted Encumbrances, sufficient to result in Austral having the interests shown in Exhibit 1.1 in each unit or well (as the case may be) in which any portion of such Title Property is included. Exhibit 1.1 accurately reflects Austral's interests (derived from its record or beneficial ownership of interests in a Title Property) in each unit or well (as the case may be) in which any portion of such Title Property is included. None of the liens, claims or encumbrances affecting any Title Property impairs in any material respect the use or value of Austral's interests in such Title Property for the purposes for which they are held. Austral has made no title investigation with respect to the Oil and Gas Properties which are not Title Properties and therefore cannot make, and nothing herein shall be construed as, any title representation with respect thereto; however, Austral has followed generally accepted industry practice in acquiring such Oil and Gas Properties. Except as set forth in Exhibit 1.1, all rentals, royalties, overriding royalties, fees or other payments due and payable under all leases and other instruments granting rights to explore for and produce Substances which are included in the Oil and Gas Properties have been fully paid (or tendered) and no overriding or other royalty interests (other than those reflected in the instruments identified on an Exhibit delivered pursuant to this Agreement or otherwise referred to in any such Exhibit) are payable with respect thereto.

5.4 *Physical Facilities and Operating Condition.* Austral or OPI, as the case may be, has good title to its interests in the machinery, plants, gathering lines and other pipelines, structures, field offices, equipment, furniture, vehicles, boats, materials, supplies and other assets described in Section 1.1.3 which constitute a portion of the Properties and which are situated on, used or held for use in connection with any Title Property, free and clear of all liens, claims or encumbrances except as set forth in Exhibit 1.1. The foregoing property, plant and equipment are in the aggregate in good repair, working order and operating condition and are adequate for the operation of the Domestic Properties as currently being operated.

5.5 *Insurance Policies.* Exhibit 5.5 lists all insurance policies and bonds in force with respect to the Domestic Properties (excepting those with respect to which Austral is not the operator) and their operations and with respect to the properties and operations of APG and shows as to each policy or bond the type of coverage, policy or bond number, issuing company, policy limit or bond amount, deductible amount (if any), annual premium, expiration date and named insured or beneficiary.

5.6 *Litigation.* Except as set forth in Exhibits 1.1, 5.6, 5.15 or 5.16, and for administrative or legislative actions, proceedings and investigations pending or threatened which relate to the taxation, regulation, deregulation, control, or operations of phases of the oil and gas industry as a whole and to which neither Austral, APG nor OPI is a party, to the knowledge of Austral there is no action, suit, proceeding (administrative or otherwise), claim, arbitration or investigation pending or threatened against, or affecting, any of the Domestic Properties, APG or OPI or questioning the validity of this Agreement in any court or before any governmental agency or instrumentality or other entity; nor are there any claims or grounds for any claim known to Austral which might result in any such action, suit, proceeding, claim, arbitration or investigation being instituted.

5.7 *No Violations of Law.* Except as set forth in Exhibits 1.1, 5.7, 5.15 or 5.16, to the knowledge of Austral, neither Austral, APG nor OPI is in violation of any provision of any law, ordinance, requirement, regulation, decree or order applicable in any material respect to any Material Property or the business of APG, including, without limitation, the rules and regulations of the Department of Energy and all governmental authorities under that department, including the Federal Energy Regulatory Commission and the Economic Regulatory Administration.

5.8 Corporate Power. The execution and delivery of this Agreement and the consummation of the transactions contemplated hereby have been duly authorized by the Board of Directors of Austral and no other corporate proceedings on the part of Austral are necessary to authorize this Agreement and the transactions contemplated hereby, except for the approval of this Agreement by the stockholders of Austral in the manner prescribed by the Delaware General Corporation Law and the adoption by the stockholders of Austral of a plan of complete liquidation of Austral pursuant to Section 337 of the Internal Revenue Code (the "Plan"), which shall provide for the distribution of Austral's assets to its stockholders as expeditiously as reasonably practicable.

5.9 No Defaults and Consummation of Transactions. Except as set forth in Exhibits 1.1 or 5.15, (i) each obligation, agreement, lease, undertaking, policy, bond, contract, easement or instrument designated as "material" by Superior on any Exhibit delivered by Austral to Superior pursuant to this Agreement and each lease or other instrument designated as a Title Property on Exhibit 1.1 ("Instrument") is in full force and effect and is, to the knowledge of Austral, a valid and legally binding obligation of the parties thereto enforceable in accordance with its terms; (ii) to the knowledge of Austral, no party to any Instrument is in material dispute with any other party thereto or is in breach or default with respect to any of its material obligations thereunder, and there has not occurred any event, fact or circumstance which with the lapse of time or the giving of notice, or both, would constitute a breach or default thereunder; (iii) to the knowledge of Austral, no party to any Instrument has given or threatened to give notice of any action to terminate, cancel, rescind or procure a judicial reformation of any Instrument; and (iv) the execution and delivery of this Agreement and the consummation of the transactions contemplated hereby, will not result in . breach or violation of, or constitute a default under the provisions of any Instrument or of any law, ordinance, requirement, regulation, decree or order applicable to Austral, the Domestic Properties, APG or OPI and will not conflict with any provision of the Certificate of Incorporation or by-laws of Austral, APG or OPI.

5.10 No Broker. Except for Lehman Brothers Kuhn Loeb Incorporated whose fees and expenses are to be paid by Austral, Austral has not employed or retained any broker or finder or paid or agreed to pay any brokerage fee or commission or any finder's fee to any broker, agent or finder on account of this Agreement or any matters contemplated hereby.

5.11 Certain Changes in Material Properties. Except as otherwise set forth in Exhibit 5.11, since September 30, 1977 the Material Properties, viewed as a whole, have not experienced any reduction in the rate of production of Substances, other than changes in the ordinary course of operation, and no Material Property has suffered any material destruction, damage or loss or, except as disclosed in Exhibit 1.1, been subjected to any undischarged mortgage, lien, charge, encumbrance, claim or security interest.

5.12 Other Contracts and Agreements. Exhibit 5.12 contains a complete list of all contracts, agreements, leases, undertakings (whether written or oral) and instruments which are not included on any other Exhibit delivered pursuant hereto, involving in each case an aggregate obligation of Austral, APG or OPI in excess of $10,000, which constitute a part of the Properties or as to which APG or OPI is a party, or by which, to the knowledge of Austral, the Domestic Properties are subject or bound.

5.13 Licenses and Permits. Exhibits 1.1, 5.13 or 5.15 reflect (i) all permits, licenses or other authorizations ("Permits") (a) which are material to the operation of any Material

Property of which Austral is the operator, (b) of which Austral has knowledge and which are material to the business and operations of APG, or (c) which are material to the business and operations of OPI, (ii) the name of the authority issuing each Permit and the name of the party to whom such Permit is issued, (iii) the issue and expiration date of each Permit and the kinds of business authorized to be conducted thereunder and (iv) each person or entity authorized thereunder to conduct such business. Each of the Permits reflected in Exhibits 1.1, 5.13 or 5.15 to Austral's knowledge is in full force and effect except as set forth in any such Exhibit.

5.14   Consolidated Financial Statements of Austral.   The consolidated balance sheets of Austral and its consolidated subsidiaries as of December 31, 1976, September 30, 1977 and December 31, 1977, and the related consolidated statements of income, stockholders' investment and changes in financial position for the three years ended December 31, 1976, the nine months ended September 30, 1976 and 1977, and the year-ended December 31, 1977, together with the notes thereto, copies of which have been furnished to Superior, have been prepared in accordance with generally accepted accounting principles consistently applied during the periods involved, and have been reported on by Arthur Andersen & Co., independent public accountants. The aforementioned financial statements present fairly the financial position of Austral and its consolidated subsidiaries as of the dates of the balance sheets, and the results of their operations and changes in their financial position for the periods then ended. Except as disclosed on Exhibits 1.1, 5.14, or 5.15, Austral and its consolidated subsidiaries did not have, on the dates of such balance sheets, any liabilities, contingent or otherwise, which are material either individually or in the aggregate, which are not reflected on such balance sheets or in the notes thereto. Since the date of the December 31, 1977 balance sheet there has been no material adverse change in the financial position, business or properties of Austral and its consolidated subsidiaries.

5.15   Petroleum Properties and Other Agreements of APG.   Exhibit 5.15 describes all leases, licenses, production sharing agreements, concessions, grants, and other rights and all farmouts and other interests therein owned or held by APG and all joint venture agreements, operating agreements and other agreements in which APG has an interest relating to the exploration, extraction, processing or marketing of Substances. APG is not a party to, nor are any of its properties bound by, and it has no knowledge of, any agreement other than those described in Exhibit 5.15 affecting or relating to APG's rights or interests under the Production Sharing Contract or the Joint Venture Agreement referred to as such on such Exhibit. APG's interests in and under such Production Sharing Contract and such Joint Venture Agreement are, except as described in Exhibit 5.15, free and clear of all liens, charges, pledges, security interests and other encumbrances. The parties to the Joint Venture Agreement are hereinafter referred to as the "Huffco Group" and are identified in Exhibit 5.15.

5.16   Financial Statements of APG.   The unaudited balance sheets of APG as of December 31, 1975 and 1976 and September 30, 1977 and the unaudited related statements of income, retained earnings and changes in financial position for the two years ended December 31, 1976 and the nine months ended September 30, 1976 and 1977, together with the notes thereto, copies of which have been furnished to Superior, have been prepared in accordance with generally accepted accounting principles consistently applied during the periods involved. Such financial statements present fairly the financial position of APG as of December 31, 1975 and 1976 and September 30, 1977, and the results of its operations and changes in financial position for the periods then ended subject to normal year-end adjustments in the case of the September 30, 1976 and 1977 statements. Except as disclosed on Exhibits 5.15 or 5.16, APG did not have, on the dates of such balance sheets, any liabilities, contingent or otherwise, which are material, either individually or in the aggregate, which are not reflected on such balance sheets or in the notes thereto. Since the date of the September 30, 1977 balance sheet there has been no material and adverse change in the financial position, business or properties of APG. Such balance sheet makes sufficient provision for the payment of all unpaid federal, state, local, foreign or other taxes, including interest or penalties of APG accrued for or applicable to the period ended on such date and all years and periods prior thereto for which APG may at such date have been liable in its own right or as transferee of the assets of, or as successor to, any other corporation.

5.17 *Absence of Certain Changes — APG.* Since September 30, 1977, APG has not, except as consented to by Superior, or as required by the documents scheduled on Exhibit 5.15 or as otherwise set forth on Exhibit 5.17:

(i) entered into any transaction or contract, commitment or agreement other than in the ordinary course of business;

(ii) sold, transferred, assigned or conveyed or agreed to sell, assign, transfer or convey any of its tangible assets other than in the ordinary course of business;

(iii) sold, transferred, assigned or conveyed any of its intangible assets, including any segment of its business; or made, or agreed or committed to make, any business acquisition, merger or combination (excluding any conveyance by APG to Austral of its insurance claims attributable to the operations of APG prior to October 1, 1977);

(iv) suffered any change in its business operations, assets, liabilities or financial condition, other than changes in the ordinary course of business which, individually and in the aggregate, are not materially adverse;

(v) suffered any material destruction, damage or loss to any of its assets or property, whether or not covered by insurance;

(vi) mortgaged or pledged or agreed to mortgage or pledge any of its assets or suffered, permitted, incurred or agreed to the imposition of any lien, charge, encumbrance or claim upon its assets, tangible or intangible, or business;

(vii) discharged, satisfied or reduced any mortgage, lien, charge or encumbrance upon its assets or business, other than as required by the terms of such mortgage, lien, charge or encumbrance;

(viii) incurred, paid or become subject to any liability, obligation or guaranty (accrued, absolute, contingent or otherwise), other than current liabilities incurred in the ordinary course of business and intercompany accounts owed by APG to Austral;

(ix) committed, suffered, permitted or incurred any default in any obligation, contract, agreement, lease, undertaking or instrument to which it is a party;

(x) made any change adverse to it in the terms of any obligation, contract, agreement, lease, undertaking or instrument;

(xi) waived, cancelled, sold or otherwise disposed of for less than the fair value thereof any claim or right against others;

(xii) declared, agreed to pay or make, or paid or made any dividend, distribution of assets of any kind or other payment in cash, stock or otherwise to its stockholder;

(xiii) written off any item reflected in its balance sheet at September 30, 1977 or written down the value of any such item except in accordance with schedules of depreciation or amortization previously established and consistently applied and except for items written off or written down against reserves previously established;

(xiv) issued or agreed to issue any shares of any class of stock, bonds or other corporate securities, redeemed, purchased or otherwise acquired any of its shares or securities, or granted or agreed to grant any options, warrants or other rights calling for the issue thereof, or made any change whatsoever in its capitalization;

(xv) changed any accounting method or practice previously followed by it;

(xvi) authorized the entering into of any transaction or agreement which is not in the ordinary course of business;

(xvii) entered into or agreed to enter into any agreement or arrangement granting any preferential rights to purchase any of the assets, properties or rights of APG or requiring the consent of any person to the transfer and assignment of such assets, properties or rights;

(xviii) made or permitted any amendment or termination of any contract, agreement or license to which it is a party; or

(xix) made capital expenditures or entered into commitments therefor, aggregating more than $25,000.

5.18   APG's Accounts Receivable.   Except as set forth in Exhibit 5.18, the accounts receivable shown on APG's balance sheet at September 30, 1977, and all accounts receivable generated since that date, constitute valid and binding obligations that arose in the ordinary course of business.

5.19   Employees of APG.   APG has no employees or salaried officers.

5.20   Banks.   Exhibit 5.20 lists all banks and other financial institutions in which APG or OPI (i) has an account or maintains a safe deposit box, showing the names of the persons authorized to act or deal in connection therewith and the account or safe deposit box numbers relating thereto or (ii) has a line of credit or letter of credit setting forth a brief description of the terms thereof.

5.21   Powers of Attorney.   Exhibit 5.21 lists all persons holding powers of attorney for APG or OPI (and for Austral, as such powers of attorney relate to the Properties) and shows the scope and term of each such power of attorney.

5.22   Tax Returns.   APG and OPI have delivered to Superior true and complete copies of all federal, state, county, municipal and foreign tax returns, reports and declarations required to be filed by them for their fiscal years ended on the last day of December 1972 through 1976. APG and OPI have timely and properly filed all federal, state, county, municipal and foreign income, profits and franchise tax returns required to be filed by them for all periods ended on or prior to the date hereof and have timely paid all federal, state, county, municipal and foreign income, profits and franchise taxes payable by them for all such periods; no assessments or notices of deficiency have been received by them with respect to any such tax or any such return; and no amendments or applications for refund have been filed or are planned with respect to any such tax or return for any such period. APG and OPI have timely paid custom duties and imposts and all sales, use, ad valorem, value added, excise, employment and similar taxes payable by them for all periods ended on or prior to the date hereof; and no assessment or notice of deficiency has been received with respect to any such tax. Except as set forth in Exhibit 5.22, no audit, inquiry, or examination has commenced, to the knowledge of Austral, for any tax return filed by APG or OPI or with respect to any tax payable by APG or OPI nor has any consent been given to waiving any statute of limitations with respect to any such return or tax. Except as reflected on the tax returns referred to in this Section 5.22, there are no outstanding elections or consents of any kind made or given by APG or OPI under any tax statute, rule or regulation.

5.23   Proxy Statement.   Information with respect to Austral, APG and OPI to be included in Austral's proxy statement to be used in connection with the special meeting of stockholders of Austral to be called in order to obtain approval of this Agreement (the "Austral Stockholders' Meeting"), including, without limitation, all information relating to the business, properties, and management of Austral, APG and OPI and all financial statements contained therein, as the Austral proxy statement may be amended or supplemented prior to the date of the Austral Stockholders' Meeting (the "Austral Proxy Statement"), will, as of the date of the Austral Stockholders' Meeting and as of the Closing Date, contain no untrue statement of a material fact or omit to state a material fact required to be stated therein or necessary to make the statements contained therein, in the light of the circumstances under which they were made, not misleading.

5.24 *Federal Leases.* Exhibit 5.24 sets forth the aggregate number, by states, of acres covered by oil and gas leases (including options for such leases or interests therein) of Austral and OPI on land held under the provisions of the Mineral Lands Leasing Act of 1920, as amended.

5.25 *No Omissions or Misrepresentations.* None of the representations or warranties made by Austral to Superior in this Agreement (including the information in any Exhibit delivered pursuant hereto) or in any certificate or document delivered to Superior pursuant to this Agreement by or on behalf of Austral, contains any untrue statement of a material fact or omits to state a material fact necessary to be stated in order to make the representations or warranties contained herein or therein not misleading. There is no fact known to Austral, and which is not otherwise known to Superior, which materially adversely affects the operation, prospects or condition of any Material Property or the business, operations, affairs, prospects or condition of APG or its properties or assets which has not been set forth in this Agreement, including the Exhibits delivered pursuant hereto.

5.26 *APG Assets.* Except as set forth in Exhibit 5.15, APG has good title to all of its material assets, free and clear of all liens, claims and encumbrances.

5.27 *Fee Simple Estates.* Except as set forth in Exhibit 1.1, Austral owns no real property in fee simple.

5.28 *Waiver of Preferential Purchase Rights.* Except as set forth in Exhibit 5.28, there exist no preferential purchase rights with respect to any Material Property which have not been waived by all persons or entities necessary for effective and valid waiver thereof.

5.29 *Substitution as Operator.* Except as set forth in Exhibit 5.29, Austral has obtained the consents of all operating committees and all nonoperators of each unit or lease of which Austral is the operator, necessary for the substitution, effective as of the Closing Date, of Superior as such operator.

6. COVENANTS OF AUSTRAL.

6.1 *Conduct of Business Pending Closing.* Austral covenants that from the date hereof to the Closing Date, except (i) as provided herein, (ii) as required by any obligation, agreement, lease, undertaking, policy, bond, contract, easement, or instrument referred to on any Exhibit hereto, (iii) as otherwise consented to by Superior, or (iv) as set forth on Exhibit 6.1, Austral will:

6.1.1 Not (i) operate or in any manner deal with, incur obligations with respect to, or undertake any transactions relating to, the Domestic Properties or to the business of APG other than in the normal, usual and customary manner and of a nature and in an amount consistent with prior practice and in the ordinary and regular course of business of owning and operating the Domestic Properties and APG and in the regular course of business of OPI; (ii) acquire, dispose of or relinquish any Oil and Gas Properties (other than relinquishments resulting from the expiration of leases which Austral has no right or option to renew); or (iii) make capital expenditures or work-over expenditures with respect to the Domestic Properties or the business of APG, except when required by an emergency when there shall have been insufficient time to obtain advance consent.

6.1.2 Use its best efforts, including but not limited to, maintaining or increasing the level of compensation and employee benefits, to keep available the services of the present employees of Austral who discharge duties with respect to the Domestic Properties, APG or OPI and to preserve relationships with all third parties having business dealings with respect to the Domestic Properties, APG or OPI.

6.1.3 Notify, as reasonably requested by Superior, all governmental regulatory authorities and cooperate with Superior in obtaining the issuance by each such authority of such permits, licenses and authorizations as may be necessary for Superior to own and operate the Properties following the consummation of the transactions contemplated herein.

6.1.4   Timely make all filings and give all notices required under all contracts relating to the Domestic Properties or the business and operations of APG, including but not limited to all filings and notices required to be filed by Austral, APG or OPI to obtain available price increases, as may be required pursuant to any contract, the failure to file or give which would materially and adversely affect the Domestic Properties and the business and operations of APG taken as a whole.

6.1.5   Proceed with calling and convening the Austral Stockholders' Meeting, such efforts to commence as soon as practicable following the execution of this Agreement.

6.1.6   Proceed with obtaining the rulings as set forth in Section 9.2.

6.1.7   Not permit APG to (i) declare or pay any dividend, in cash, stock or otherwise, or make any distribution or payment in respect of its capital stock, or directly or indirectly redeem or purchase or otherwise acquire any of its capital stock, or authorize any such payment, distribution, redemption or purchase or (ii) amend, repeal or otherwise alter the Certificate of Incorporation or by-laws of APG.

6.1.8   Subject to the provisions of Section 12.14, continue to make available to Superior's personnel, accountants and attorneys in Austral's offices true, complete and current documents, records and files pertaining to the Domestic Properties and to the business and operations of APG and OPI, and continue to provide facilities for copying such documents and continue to make available at Superior's request knowledgeable Austral personnel or representatives to assist Superior in its review of such documents and files.

6.2   *FPC Refunds.*   Moneys collected by Austral for gas sales subject to refund under orders of the Department of Energy or any component thereof (including the Federal Energy Regulatory Commission) and the Federal Energy Administration and any predecessor governmental agency that may be payable to royalty owners, overriding royalty owners and working interest owners other than Austral and which are held by Austral on the Closing Date, will be paid by Austral to Superior no later than the date of the submission of the Closing Statement, accompanied by complete lists (to the extent known by Austral) of payees' names, addresses, social security numbers, taxpayers' identification numbers and applicable amounts by month and by lease.

6.3   *Royalty and Other Payments.*   Moneys collected by Austral for the sale of Substances that are payable to royalty owners, overriding royalty owners and working interest owners and are held in suspense on the Closing Date will be paid by Austral to Superior no later than the date of submission of the Closing Statement, accompanied by a complete list (to the extent known by Austral) of the amounts by month for each property, and each owner, to the extent applicable.

6.4   *Additional Disclosures and Information.*   Austral shall give Superior prompt notice if at any time on or prior to the Closing Date there is (or as to past acts or events, it discovers) a change in any state of facts, or there is the occurrence, non-occurrence or existence of any event either prior or subsequent to the date of this Agreement, which change or event is known to Austral and which would make any representation or warranty (including the information set forth in the Exhibits delivered pursuant to this Agreement) made by Austral to Superior not true and correct in all material respects, it being the intention of Austral and Superior that Austral shall engage in a continuous disclosure process from the date of this Agreement through the Closing Date. Any such information delivered to Superior by Austral pursuant thereto shall be deemed a supplement to and modification of the representation and warranty to which it relates. Where appropriate an Exhibit or an amended Exhibit shall be promptly prepared and delivered to Superior and copies of any relevant documents shall be delivered to Superior.

6.5 *Good Standing Certificates.*   Prior to the Closing, Austral shall deliver to Superior certificates from Secretaries of State and appropriate state taxing authorities, or other evidence acceptable to Superior, evidencing the current incorporation or qualification, good standing and payment of all requisite franchise taxes of Austral, APG and OPI in each jurisdiction where any of such corporations are incorporated or qualified to do business as a foreign corporation.

7. REPRESENTATIONS AND WARRANTIES BY SUPERIOR.   Superior represents and warrants as follows:

7.1 *Organization and Corporate Power.*   Superior is a corporation duly organized, validly existing, and in good standing under the laws of the State of Nevada and has all requisite corporate power and authority to acquire and own the Properties and to enter into this Agreement and to carry out the transactions contemplated hereby. Superior is qualified to do business as a foreign corporation and is in good standing in all states and jurisdictions in which Properties are located and wherein Superior is required to be so qualified.

7.2 *Due Authorization.*   The execution and delivery of this Agreement and the consummation of the transactions contemplated hereby have been duly authorized by the Board of Directors of Superior and no other corporate proceedings on the part of Superior are necessary to authorize this Agreement and the transactions contemplated hereby.

7.3 *Consummation of Transactions.*   The execution and delivery of this Agreement and the consummation of the transactions contemplated hereby will not result in a breach or violation of, or constitute a default under the provisions of any agreement or other instrument to which Superior is a party or by which Superior or its properties are bound or affected or of any law, ordinance, requirement, regulation, decree or order applicable to Superior or its properties, and will not conflict with any provisions of Superior's Articles of Incorporation or bylaws. Without limiting the foregoing, (i) Superior has no reason to believe that it is not a qualified assignee of the federal, state, Indian and other governmental oil and gas leases and interests therein or related thereto constituting a part of the Domestic Properties, and (ii) the acquisition of the Domestic Properties and the consummation of the transactions contemplated hereby will not result in any violation of the Mineral Lands Leasing Act of 1920, as amended, or of any related rules and regulations.

7.4 *No Broker.*   Superior has not employed or retained any broker or finder or paid or agreed to pay any brokerage fee or commission or any finder's fee to any broker, agent or finder on account of this Agreement or any matters contemplated hereby.

7.5 *Preservation of Books and Records of Austral, APG and OPI.*   For a period of ten years from the Closing Date, Superior will preserve the books and records of Austral, APG and OPI delivered to it pursuant hereto and will make such books and records available to Austral upon reasonable notice at Superior's administrative headquarters in Houston, Texas, or such other location in the States of Texas or Louisiana as Superior shall advise Austral in writing, at reasonable times during regular office hours.

7.6 *Proxy Statement.*   Superior shall promptly furnish to Austral all information that Austral may reasonably request for inclusion in the Austral Proxy Statement and any such information included with the concurrence of Superior in the Austral Proxy Statement as it may be amended or supplemented prior to the date of the Austral Stockholders' Meeting shall as of the date of the Austral Stockholders' Meeting and as of the Closing Date contain no untrue statement of a material fact or omit to state a material fact required to be stated therein or necessary to make the statements contained therein, in light of the circumstances under which they were made, not misleading.

7.7 *Investment Representation.*   Superior is acquiring the APG Stock for investment for its own account and not with a view to the distribution or resale thereof, and by its consummation of the transactions contemplated hereby Superior reaffirms this representation and warranty.

7.8 *No Omissions or Misrepresentations.* None of the representations or warranties made by Superior to Austral in this Agreement, or in any certificate or document delivered to Austral pursuant to this Agreement by or on behalf of Superior, contains any untrue statement of a material fact or omits to state a material fact necessary to be stated in order to make the representations or warranties contained herein or therein not misleading.

7.9 *Other Representations.* Superior will refrain from taking any action and will not suffer any inaction by it which would render nugatory any tax rulings of the Internal Revenue Service relating to annual or continuing general oil and gas programs sponsored by Austral and its subsidiaries from 1951 through 1970, which rulings are more particularly identified in Exhibit 7.9 hereto.

8.   Conditions Precedent to Obligations of Superior. All obligations of Superior under this Agreement are, at its election, subject to the satisfaction, prior to or at the Closing, of each of the following conditions:

8.1 *Accuracy of Representations.* The representations and warranties of Austral set forth in this Agreement (including the information in the Exhibits hereto) (i) shall have been true and correct in all material respects on the date of this Agreement, and (ii) as supplemented and modified pursuant to Section 6.4, shall be true and correct in all material respects as of the Closing Date with the same effect as though made at such date. No change in the representations and warranties of Austral as disclosed in any supplemented or modified Exhibit or in any other information delivered to Superior pursuant to Section 6.4 between the date of this Agreement and the Closing Date shall reflect a change in any state of facts, or the occurrence, non-occurrence or existence of any events (whether individually or in the aggregate) which shall have a material adverse effect on the Domestic Properties and the business and operations of APG taken as a whole. Austral shall have performed and complied in all material respects with all covenants and conditions required by this Agreement to be performed or complied with by it prior to or as of the Closing Date and shall have delivered to Superior a certificate dated the Closing Date and signed by its Chairman or President and Secretary or Assistant Secretary certifying to the fulfillment of the foregoing conditions.

8.2 *Stockholder Approval.* At the meeting of the stockholders of Austral provided for herein, the Plan shall have been adopted by the stockholders of Austral by the affirmative vote required under Austral's Certificate of Incorporation and by-laws and applicable law, thereby also constituting specific authorization by such stockholders of this Agreement and all transactions contemplated herein.

8.3 *Opinion of Counsel of Austral.* There shall be delivered to Superior an opinion of counsel to Austral, Messrs. Vinson & Elkins, addressed to Superior and dated the Closing Date substantially in form and substance as set forth in Exhibit 8.3.

8.4 *Opinion of Special Indonesian Counsel.* There shall be delivered to Superior an opinion of special Indonesian counsel to Austral and Superior, Messrs. Mochtar, Karuwin & Komar, addressed to Superior and Austral and dated as of the Closing Date substantially in form and substance as set forth in Exhibit 8.4.

8.5 *No Pending Suits.* At the Closing Date, no suit, action or other proceeding shall be pending or threatened before any court or governmental agency in which it is sought to restrain or prohibit the performance of or to obtain damages or other relief in connection with this Agreement or the consummation of the transactions contemplated hereby.

8.6 *Consents.* Austral shall have obtained (i) the unqualified consents of the Minister of Mines on behalf of the Government of the Republic of Indonesia and Perusahaan Pertambangan Minyak Dan Gas Bumi Negara ("Pertamina"), a State Enterprise of the Republic of Indonesia, to the transfer of the APG Stock to Superior, (ii) all other consents, waivers and releases, including, without limitation, those of Bankers Trust Company and all other members of the Huffco Group, which are necessary to transfer the APG Stock to Superior and (iii) all consents which are necessary to assign to Superior the domestic gas sales contracts constituting a part of the Domestic Properties. Austral shall have used its best efforts to obtain all other consents, waivers and releases which are necessary, desirable or appropriate to effectuate the transactions contemplated by this Agreement; however, the failure to obtain any such consents, waivers, or releases, and the resultant failure, if any, to transfer to Superior any related property, shall not be deemed (i) to result in a breach of any representation, warranty, covenant or agreement made by Austral hereunder or pursuant hereto or in connection with the transactions contemplated hereby, (ii) to result in any liability of Austral to Superior, or (iii) except as provided for in Section 8.9 to create a right in Superior to terminate this Agreement.

8.7 *Comfort Letter.* Arthur Andersen & Co. shall have furnished to Superior a letter dated as of the Closing Date, in form and substance satisfactory to Superior, confirming that on the basis of carrying out certain specified procedures (but not an examination in accordance with generally accepted auditing standards), which procedures included a reading of the latest available interim unaudited consolidated financial statements of Austral and the interim unaudited financial statements of APG, a reading of the minutes of the meetings of the stockholders and directors of Austral and APG and inquiries of certain officers of Austral and APG who have responsibility for financial and accounting matters, nothing has come to their attention which has caused them to believe that:

(i) The unaudited financial statements referred to in Section 5.16 do not fairly present in conformity with generally accepted accounting principles applied consistently during the periods involved the financial position of APG or the results of operations of APG, for the periods indicated.

(ii) With respect to the periods subsequent to September 30, 1977 in the case of APG and the period subsequent to December 31, 1977 in the case of Austral, there were, at a specified date not more than five days prior to the date of the letter, (a) any changes in the capital stock or increase in the long term debt or any decrease in excess of $100,000 in the net assets of APG; (b) any decreases in the carrying value of Austral's domestic and APG's foreign oil and gas properties, other than decreases resulting from depletion, depreciation and amortization in accordance with previously established policies, which in the aggregate are material to the Properties; (c) any increase in the liabilities of Austral for the advance sale of Substances to be delivered in the future except in accordance with the terms of the Advance Sale Agreement; and (d) any material decrease, as compared with the corresponding period in the preceding year, in APG's total revenues, income before taxes and extraordinary items or net income of APG.

8.8 *Substitution of Superior as Operator.* Austral shall have used its best efforts to obtain all requisite consents of any operating committees and all non-operators of each unit or lease of which Austral is the operator, to the substitution, effective as of the Closing Date, of Superior as such operator, and Austral shall have resigned, effective as of the Closing Date, from each unit or lease constituting part of the Properties of which it is the operator.

8.9 *Title Adjustment.* The Title Adjustment shall be an amount not more than $5,000,000.

8.10 *Resignation of Officers and Directors.* Superior shall have received the written resignations of all officers and directors of APG and OPI (other than directors of OPI representing the University of Texas Ex-Students' Association) and all representatives of either corporation or Austral serving on operating or other committees relating to the management of any Domestic Property or the Joint Venture referred to in Section 5.15, such resignations to be effective on or before the Closing Date.

8.11 *Preferential Purchase Right.* Austral shall have assigned its preferential right to purchase the OPI Stock to Superior.

8.12 *Non-exclusive License.* Austral-Erwin Engineering Company, a Delaware corporation ("Austral-Erwin"), shall have delivered to Superior a non-exclusive, non-transferable, royalty-free license substantially in the form of Exhibit 8.12, permitting Superior, any of Superior's majority-owned subsidiaries and Canadian Superior Oil Ltd. (so long as Superior owns at least 45% of the capital stock of such company) to make or have made and to use in their business, but not to sell, any and all of the inventions covered by the existing United States patents and presently pending United States patent applications (as well as any United States patents which may subsequently issue thereon) of Austral-Erwin.

8.13 *Opinion Respecting Indonesian Operations.* Superior shall have received from Messrs. Baker & Botts, special counsel for APG and the other members of the Huffco Group in respect of the Production Sharing Contract referred to in Section 5.15 and certain agreements related thereto, and operations conducted thereunder, an opinion stating that except as disclosed therein or in Exhibit 5.15 they know of no pending or threatened litigation, action or proceeding which could have a material adverse effect on the business, properties or results of operations of APG and the rights and benefits vested in APG under the Production Sharing Contract referred to in Section 5.15.

8.14 *Opinions Respecting Certain Conveyancing Documents.* There shall be delivered to Superior from special counsel in each state where Title Properties are located (other than Texas and Louisiana) an opinion, satisfactory in form and substance to Superior, to the effect that the form of each conveyance delivered by Austral to Superior pursuant to Sections 10.2.1, 10.2.3 and 10.2.4 which relate to Properties located in such state is in a form effective to convey the Properties referred to therein in the manner provided for therein, and upon due authorization, execution and delivery by the parties thereto, will constitute a legal, valid and binding conveyance of Austral enforceable in accordance with its terms. Such counsel need not express any title opinion or opinion with respect to the laws of any jurisdiction other than its own with respect to the Properties referred to in any such conveyance.

9. CONDITIONS PRECEDENT TO OBLIGATIONS OF AUSTRAL. All obligations of Austral under this Agreement are, at its election, subject to the satisfaction on or prior to the Closing Date of each of the following conditions:

9.1 *Accuracy of Representations.* The representations and warranties of Superior contained herein shall be true and correct in all material respects as of the Closing Date with the same effect as though made at such date, except as permitted by this Agreement. Superior shall have performed and complied in all material respects with all covenants and conditions required by this Agreement to be performed or complied with by it prior to or as of the Closing Date and shall have delivered to Austral a certificate dated the Closing Date and signed by its President or any Vice President and its Secretary or any Assistant Secretary certifying to the fulfillment of the foregoing conditions.

9.2 *Tax Rulings.* Austral shall have received from the Internal Revenue Service favorable rulings satisfactory to it in form and substance and to the effect that (i) for purposes of Section 337 of the Internal Revenue Code, the Plan will be a plan of complete liquidation and the date of adoption of the Plan will be the date the Plan is approved by the stockholders of Austral; (ii) if all the assets of Austral (except property retained to meet claims, including unascertained or contingent liabilities, liabilities arising from or under agreements of sale, and liquidation expenses) are distributed in complete liquidation within the 12-month period beginning on the date of adoption of the Plan as provided by the Plan, no gain or loss will be recognized by Austral upon the sale of its assets except for certain items of recapture with respect to depreciable assets; (iii) no gain or loss will be recognized by Austral upon the distribution of its assets pursuant to the Plan; (iv) amounts distributed by Austral to its stockholders in complete liquidation will be treated as full payment in exchange for their stock so that any gain or loss realized by the stockholders will constitute capital gain or loss to all stockholders in whose hands the stock is a capital asset; (v) the liquidating trust utilized in connection with the Plan will be classified as a trust for Federal income tax purposes and not as an association taxable as a corporation and the former stockholders of Austral will be treated as the owners of such trust; (vi) the sale by Superior of 25,000 shares of Austral Common Stock and the warrant to purchase 240,000 shares of Austral Stock prior to the signing of the Agreement will be treated as an independent transaction, separate and distinct from the proposed liquidation of Austral; and (vii) for purposes of Section 337 of the Internal Revenue Code, Austral will not be considered a collapsible corporation with respect to any sale or exchange by it within the twelve-month period beginning on the date of adoption of the Plan.

9.3 *Opinion of Counsel of Superior.* There shall be delivered to Austral an opinion of counsel of Superior, Messrs. Bracewell & Patterson, addressed to Austral and dated the Closing Date substantially in form and substance as set forth in Exhibit 9.3.

9.4 *No Pending Suits.* At the Closing Date, no suit, action or other proceeding shall be pending or threatened before any court or governmental agency in which it is sought to restrain or prohibit the performance of or to obtain damages or other relief in connection with this Agreement or the consummation of the transactions contemplated hereby.

9.5 *Stockholder Approval.* At the meeting of the stockholders of Austral provided for herein, the Plan shall have been adopted by the stockholders of Austral by the affirmative vote required under Austral's Certificate of Incorporation and by-laws and applicable law, thereby also constituting specific authorization by such stockholders of this Agreement and all transactions contemplated herein.

9.6 *Opinion of Special Indonesian Counsel.* There shall be delivered to Austral an opinion of special Indonesian counsel to Austral and Superior, Messrs. Mochtar, Karuwin & Komar, addressed to Austral and Superior and dated as of the Closing Date substantially in form and substance as set forth in Exhibit 8.4.

9.7 *Consents.* Austral shall have obtained (i) the unqualified consents of the Minister of Mines on behalf of the Government of the Republic of Indonesia and Pertamina to transfer the APG Stock to Superior, (ii) all other consents, waivers and releases, including, without limitation, those of Bankers Trust Company and all other members of the Huffco Group, which are necessary to transfer the APG Stock to Superior, and (iii) all consents which are necessary to assign to Superior the domestic gas sales contracts constituting a part of the Domestic Properties.

9.8 *Fairness Report.* Austral shall have received a written report from Lehman Brothers Kuhn Loeb Incorporated in form and substance satisfactory to Austral to the effect that the transactions contemplated by this Agreement and by the Plan are fair to Austral's stockholders.

9.9 *Title Adjustment.* The Title Adjustment shall be an amount not more than $5,000,000.

9.10 *No Impediment to Closing.* Superior shall have delivered to Austral on the date of the Austral Stockholders' Meeting, no later than one hour prior to the commencement thereof, a certificate signed by its President or any Vice President and its Secretary or any Assistant Secretary certifying that Superior has no reason to believe that all conditions precedent to Superior's obligations hereunder have not been or will not be fulfilled in accordance with the conditions and terms of this Agreement.

10.   CLOSING AND SECOND CLOSING.

10.1 *The Closing.* The initial closing of the transactions provided for in this Agreement (the "Closing") shall be held at the offices of Messrs. Vinson & Elkins, First City National Bank Building, Houston, Texas, at 9:00 a.m. Houston time on the business day next following the day of the approval of this Agreement by the stockholders of Austral or such other time and date as shall be agreed to by Austral and Superior (the "Closing Date").

10.2 *Conveyances at the Closing.* Subject to the terms and conditions of this Agreement, on the Closing Date, Austral will grant, bargain, sell, convey, transfer, assign and deliver, and Superior will acquire from Austral, all the Properties. To effect such sale and delivery, Austral will on the Closing Date deliver to Superior the following:

10.2.1   Assignments of leases and related interests, substantially in the forms of Exhibit 10.2.1(a), Exhibit 10.2.1(b) or Exhibit 10.2.1(c) conveying all leasehold interests in and appurtenances to Oil and Gas Properties held of record by Austral.

10.2.2   Additional assignments of federal, state and Indian leases constituting a part of the Properties in the form prescribed by law in the event that a particular form of assignment is prescribed by law.

10.2.3   An assignment substantially in the form of Exhibit 10.2.3 conveying all of Austral's beneficial interest in and to all leasehold interests in and appurtenances to Oil and Gas Properties held of record by OPI and assigning the contractual rights and arrangements conferred upon Austral as operating agent for certain co-owners referred to in Section 1.3.

10.2.4   Deeds of real property fees and other interests (other than those referred to in Sections 10.2.1, 10.2.2 and 10.2.3) substantially in the form of Exhibit 10.2.4 conveying all such interests in real property held of record by Austral constituting a part of the Properties.

10.2.5   An assignment of the APG Stock, assigning such stock free and clear of all liens, claims or encumbrances except the Pledge.

10.2.6   General conveyance, transfer and assignment substantially in the form of Exhibit 10.2.6 conveying all of the Properties.

10.2.7   Specific conveyances, transfers and assignments in form and substance satisfactory to Superior and Austral of other assets constituting a part of the Properties which require specific assignment in the judgment of Superior, including without limitation, all intercompany accounts owed by APG to Austral and Austral's preferential right to purchase the OPI Stock.

10.2.8   The Transferred Records.

10.2.9   Copies of instruments evidencing all releases, consents and waivers obtained by Austral in connection with the transactions contemplated hereby.

10.2.10   All corporate books and records, including without limitation, minute books, stock transfer books, stock records and other documents, contracts, agreements, files and instruments of every kind and description of APG and OPI.

10.2.11   All such other instruments as shall be reasonably requested by Superior to vest fully in Superior title in and to the Properties as contemplated hereby.

10.3 *Consideration at the Closing.* Subject to the terms and conditions of this Agreement and against delivery of the documents described in Section 10.2, Superior shall pay to Austral on the Closing Date the Basic Price, in U.S. Dollars in immediately available funds. Superior will assume and agree to pay, perform and discharge the liabilities and obligations set forth in Section 2. The assumption of such liabilities and obligations shall be evidenced by an instrument substantially in the form of Exhibit 10.3 to be executed and delivered at the Closing.

10.4 *Receipts After Closing.* After the Closing Austral may receive funds, proceeds, contributions, refunds, rebates, payments or receipts which are attributable to the Properties after 7:00 a.m. on the Closing Date. Austral agrees to remit any of the foregoing to Superior promptly upon receipt. After the Closing, Austral may receive invoices, bills, statements and other claims for costs attributable to the Properties after 7:00 a.m. on the Closing Date. Any of the foregoing received by Austral will be promptly forwarded to Superior. Superior agrees to pay all such invoices, bills, statements and other claims forwarded by Austral or received directly by it.

10.5 *Matters Arising After Second Closing.* Austral and Superior recognize that subsequent to the Second Closing Austral may receive funds of the nature referred to in Sections 3.1.2(i) and 3.1.2(ii) and either Austral or Superior may receive invoices, bills, statements and other claims for costs of the nature referred to in Section 3.1.1(ii) for which allowances were not made in the determination of the Purchase Price. Any such funds received by Austral will be promptly remitted to Superior. Any such invoices, bills, statements and other claims received by Austral will be promptly forwarded to Superior. Superior agrees to pay all such invoices, bills, statements and other claims forwarded by Austral or received directly by it and to indemnify and hold Austral harmless with respect thereto. Any dispute between Austral and Superior relating to the propriety of the disposition of any funds or invoices, bills, statements and other claims referred to herein shall be resolved in accordance with the arbitration procedures provided for in Section 3.2.

10.6 *Additional Payment at Closing.* Upon consummation of the transactions provided for herein on the Closing Date Austral shall pay to Superior $795,000 in immediately available funds.

10.7 *Second Closing.* A second closing (the "Second Closing") shall be held at the offices of Messrs. Vinson & Elkins, First City National Bank Building, Houston, Texas, at 9:00 a.m. Houston time on the first business day next preceding the 120th day after the Closing Date, or at such other time and date as shall be agreed to by Austral and Superior, but no later than the Expiration Date, as herein defined (the "Second Closing Date"). In the event that the Purchase Price is more than the Basic Price, Superior shall pay to Austral at the Second Closing an amount equal to the Purchase Price determined in accordance with Sections 3.1 and 3.2 less the Basic Price. In the event that the Purchase Price is less than the Basic Price, Austral shall refund at the Second Closing the excess amount paid by Superior at the Closing. Said payment, if any, and the amount paid and the assumption of liabilities and obligations at the Closing, shall be the sole consideration to be paid for the Properties. All payments at the Second Closing shall be made in U.S. Dollars in immediately available funds.

11. INDEMNIFICATION.

11.1 *Survival of Covenants, Agreements, Representations and Warranties.* All covenants, agreements, representations and warranties made by Austral and Superior hereunder or pursuant hereto or in connection with the transactions contemplated hereby shall survive the Closing Date.

11.2 *Indemnification of Superior.* Austral from and after the Closing shall indemnify and hold Superior harmless from and against any and all damage, loss, cost, expense, obligation, claim or liability, including reasonable attorneys' fees ("Damages"), suffered by Superior in excess of $100,000 as a result of (i) any liability of Austral which was not to be expressly assumed by Superior pursuant to Section 2 hereof, (ii) failure of Austral or Superior to comply with the bulk sales laws of Texas or any other jurisdiction in connection with the transactions provided for herein, (iii) any brokers' or finders' fees or commissions arising from or relating to brokers or finders retained or engaged by Austral and resulting from or relating to the transactions contemplated hereby, and (iv) the breach of, or failure to perform or satisfy any of, the representations, warranties, covenants and agreements made by Austral in or under this Agreement. Austral's obligation to indemnify Superior hereunder shall be only with respect to (i) any Damages as a result of the breach of the representations in Section 5.3 with respect to Specified Material Properties for which demand is made pursuant to Section 11.4 prior to the expiration of 90 days after the Closing and (ii) any other Damages for which demand is made pursuant to Section 11.4 prior to the first business day of the eleventh calendar month after the month in which the Plan is adopted by Austral's stockholders ("Expiration Date"). Austral's obligation to indemnify Superior with respect to any Damages other than those as a result of the breach of the representations in Section 5.3 with respect to Specified Material Properties shall in no event exceed $4,000,000 in the aggregate and Austral's obligation to indemnify Superior with respect to any Damages as a result of the breach of the representations in Section 5.3 with respect to Specified Material Properties shall in no event exceed $10,000,000 in the aggregate; provided, however, that Austral's obligation to indemnify Superior with respect to all Damages hereunder shall in no event exceed $10,000,000 in the aggregate.

11.3   *Indemnification of Austral.* Superior shall indemnify and hold Austral harmless from and against any Damages suffered by Austral in excess of $100,000 as a result of the breach of, or failure to perform or satisfy any of, the representations, warranties, covenants and agreements made by Superior in this Agreement. Superior's obligation to indemnify Austral hereunder (but not otherwise) shall only be with respect to any Damages for which demand is made pursuant to Section 11.4 prior to the Expiration Date. Superior's obligation to indemnify Austral hereunder (but not otherwise) with respect to all Damages shall in no event exceed $4,000,000 in the aggregate.

11.4   *Demands, Etc.* Each indemnified party hereunder agrees that promptly upon its discovery of facts giving rise to a claim for indemnity under the provisions of this Agreement, including receipt by it of notice of any demand, assertion, claim, action or proceeding, judical or otherwise, by any third party (such third party actions being collectively referred to herein as the "Claim"), with respect to any matter as to which it is entitled to indemnity under the provisions of this Agreement, it will give prompt notice thereof in writing to the indemnifying party together with a statement of such information respecting any of the foregoing as it shall then have. Such notice shall include a formal demand for indemnification under this Agreement and shall be accompanied by an opinion of counsel to such indemnified party that such demand is not without merit under this Agreement. The indemnifying party shall not be obligated to indemnify the indemnified party with respect to any Claim if the indemnified party failed to notify the indemnifying party thereof in accordance with the provisions of this Agreement in sufficient time to permit the indemnifying party or its counsel to defend against such matter, and to make a timely response thereto including, without limitation, to prepare and assert an answer or other responsive motion to a complaint, petition, notice or other legal, equitable or administrative process relating to the Claim.

11.5   *Right to Contest and Defend.* The indemnifying party is entitled at its cost and expense to contest and defend by all appropriate legal proceedings any Claim with respect to which it is called upon to indemnify the indemnified party under the provisions of this Agreement; provided, however, that notice of the intention so to contest shall be delivered by the indemnifying party to the indemnified party within 20 days from the date of mailing to the indemnifying party of notice by the indemnified party of the assertion of the Claim. Any such contest may be conducted in the name and on behalf of the indemnifying party or the indemnified party as may be appropriate Such contest shall be conducted by reputable attorneys employed by the indemnifying party, but the indemnified party shall have the right to participate in such proceedings and to be represented by attorneys of its own choosing at its cost and expense. If the indemnified party joins in any such contest, the indemnifying party shall have full authority to determine all action to be taken with respect thereto. If after such opportunity, the indemnifying party does not elect to contest any such Claim, the indemnifying party shall be bound by the result obtained with respect thereto by the indemnified party. At any time after the commencement of defense of any Claim, the indemnifying party may request the indemnified party to agree in writing to the abandonment of such contest or to the payment or compromise by the indemnifying party of the asserted Claim, whereupon such action shall be taken unless the indemnified party so determines that the contest should be continued, and so notifies the indemnifying party in writing within 15 days of such request from the indemnifying party. In the event that the indemnified party determines that the contest should be continued, the indemnifying party shall be liable hereunder only to the extent of the lesser of (i) the amount which the other party to the contested Claim had agreed to accept in payment or compromise as of the time the indemnifying party made its request therefor to the indemnified party or (ii) such amount for which the indemnifying party may be liable with respect to such Claim by reason of the provisions hereof.

   11.6   *Cooperation.* If requested by the indemnifying party, the indemnified party agrees to cooperate with the indemnifying party and its counsel in contesting any Claim which the indemnifying party elects to contest or, if appropriate, in making any counterclaim against the person asserting the Claim, or any cross-complaint against any person, but the indemnifying party will reimburse the indemnified party for any expenses incurred by it in so cooperating.

   11.7   *Right to Participate.* The indemnified party agrees to afford the indemnifying party and its counsel the opportunity to be present at, and to participate in, conferences with all persons, including governmental authorities, asserting any Claim against the indemnified party or conferences with representatives of or counsel for such persons.

   11.8   *Payment of Damages.* The indemnifying party shall pay to the indemnified party in cash the amount of any Damages to which the indemnified party may become entitled by reason of the provisions of this Agreement, such payment to be made within five days after any such amount of Damages is finally determined either by mutual agreement of the parties hereto or pursuant to the final unappealable judgment of a court of competent jurisdiction.

   11.9   *Exclusive Remedy.* Subject to the terms, conditions and limitations contained in this Section 11, the indemnification provided hereunder shall be the exclusive remedy available (i) to Austral for the redress of any Damages as a result of the breach of, or failure to perform or satisfy any of, the representations, warranties, covenants and agreements made in this Agreement (but not otherwise) by Superior and (ii) to Superior for redress of any Damages as a result of (a) any liability of Austral which was not to be expressly assumed by Superior pursuant to Section 2 hereof, (b) failure of Austral or Superior to comply with the bulk sales laws of Texas or any other jurisdiction in connection with the transactions provided for herein, (c) any brokers' or finders' fees or commissions arising with respect to brokers or finders retained or engaged by Austral and resulting from or relating to the transactions contemplated hereby, or (d) the breach of, or failure to perform or satisfy any of, the representations, warranties, covenants and agreements made by Austral in or under this Agreement or pursuant hereto or otherwise in connection with the transactions contemplated hereby.

12.   MISCELLANEOUS PROVISIONS.

   12.1   *Termination of Agreement.* If any condition precedent to Austral's obligations hereunder is not satisfied and such condition is not waived by Austral at or prior to the Closing Date, or if any condition precedent to Superior's obligations hereunder is not satisfied and such condition is not waived by Superior at or prior to the Closing Date, Austral or Superior, as the case may be, may terminate this Agreement at its option, at or prior to the Closing, by notice to the other party. Either party may terminate this Agreement if the acquisition of the Properties has not been consummated prior to April 30, 1978, unless such date is extended by mutual agreement of Austral and Superior. This Agreement may be terminated by mutual consent of Austral and Superior at any time. Termination of this Agreement pursuant to any provision of this Section 12.1 may be effected without approval of the stockholders of Austral or Superior, either before or after the Austral Stockholders' Meeting, except as otherwise expressly provided herein. In the event of the termination of this Agreement by either party as above provided, neither of the parties shall have any liability hereunder of any nature whatsoever to the other, including any liability for damages. In the event that either party knows that a condition precedent to its obligations is not met, or that a representation or warranty to it is not true or correct in all material respects as provided for herein, nothing contained herein shall be deemed to require such party to terminate this Agreement; but in the event that such party does not terminate this Agreement, such party shall proceed with the Closing and thereby waive such condition precedent or such untrue or incorrect representation or warranty, and there shall be no liability hereunder of any nature whatsoever to the other party including any liability for damages with respect to such nonfulfillment of such condition or such untrue or incorrect representation or warranty.

12.2 *Amendment and Waiver.* Any of the terms or conditions in this Agreement may be waived by the party which is entitled to the benefit thereof by action taken by the Board of Directors of such party, or any committee or officer duly authorized or appointed by such Board of Directors for that purpose, and to the extent permitted by law this Agreement may be amended or modified in whole or in part by an agreement in writing executed in the same manner as this Agreement; provided, however, that no such agreement or modification shall include any change materially and adversely affecting the rights of the stockholders of Austral without first resubmitting any such agreement or modification to them for their approval and consent.

12.3 *Governing Law.* This Agreement shall be governed by and construed in accordance with the laws of the State of Texas. The validity of the various conveyances affecting the title to real property shall be governed by and construed in accordance with the laws of the jurisdiction in which such property is situated. The representations and warranties contained in such conveyances and the remedies arising from such representations and warranties shall be governed by and construed in accordance with the laws of the State of Texas.

12.4 *Assignment of Agreement.* Neither this Agreement nor any of the rights, benefits or obligations hereunder may be assigned by Austral without the prior written consent of Superior or by Superior without the prior written consent of Austral, except that Superior agrees that Austral may assign any or all of its rights, benefits and obligations hereunder and in connection herewith to any trust or trustees in connection with the Plan and that thereupon such trust or trustees shall have such rights, benefits and obligations and Austral shall no longer have such rights, benefits or obligations hereunder or in connection herewith. Subject to the foregoing, this Agreement shall be binding upon and inure to the benefit of the parties hereto and their respective successors and assigns; and no other person shall have any right, benefit or obligation hereunder. In addition, the representations contained in Section 7.9 shall be for the benefit of the co-owners referred to in Section 1.3.

12.5 *Publicity.* All notices to third parties and all other publicity or releases issued at or prior to the Closing concerning this Agreement and the transactions contemplated hereby shall be approved prior to release or other dissemination by both Superior and Austral.

12.6 *Notices.* Any notice, request, instruction or other document to be given hereunder by either party to the other shall be in writing, and delivered personally or mailed by registered mail, postage prepaid, as follows:

If to Superior, addressed to:

> The Superior Oil Company
> Attention: Charles L. Barney, Vice President
> 2600 First City National Bank Building
> Houston, Texas 77002

If to Austral, addressed to:

> Austral Oil Company Incorporated
> Attention: Paul R. Cole, President
> 2700 Exxon Building
> Houston, Texas 77002;

or to such other place and with such other copies as either party may designate as to itself by written notice to the other.

12.7 *Certain Taxes.* Any sales, use, gross receipts, transfer, stamp, document and other excise taxes resulting from the transfer of the Properties as provided herein shall be borne by Superior and Austral as provided by law.

12.8 *Entire Agreement.* This Agreement, together with all Exhibits hereto, constitutes the entire agreement between the parties pertaining to the subject matter hereof and supersedes all prior and contemporaneous agreements, understandings, negotiations and discussions, whether oral or written, of the parties, and there are no warranties, representations or other agreements between the parties in connection with the subject matter hereof except as set forth specifically herein or contemplated hereby.

12.9 *Austral's Assets After the Closing.* Austral agrees that it or its liquidating trust will retain, until the Second Closing, unencumbered assets having a fair market value at the Closing Date of not less than $9,000,000, and between the Second Closing and the Expiration Date, $4,000,000, in cash or in United States government securities or bank certificates of deposit. Of the amount to be held until the Second Closing, $5,000,000 shall be held for the satisfaction of any claims of Superior for refund pursuant to Section 10.7 and $4,000,000 shall be held for the satisfaction of any claims of Superior for indemnification pursuant to Section 11. All of the amount to be held between the Second Closing and the Expiration Date shall be held for the satisfaction of any claims of Superior for indemnification pursuant to Section 11.

12.10 *Further Assurances.* Each of the parties hereto shall execute and deliver to the other party hereto such other instruments as may be reasonably required in connection with the performance of this Agreement and the realization of the benefits hereof. Without limiting the generality of the foregoing, each of the parties hereto shall cooperate in obtaining all Governmental Consents; provided, however, that Austral may, in its sole discretion at any time after the Expiration Date, take such action, including making or giving of releases and relinquishments, as it deems necessary to divest itself fully of all of its right, title and interest in any Domestic Property with respect to which a Governmental Consent has not been obtained in connection with the transactions contemplated hereby or any previous transactions, and Superior agrees to do any and all things required by Austral in connection with any such divestment.

12.11 *Multiple Counterparts.* This Agreement may be executed in one or more counterparts, each of which shall be deemed an original, but all of which together shall constitute one and the same instrument.

12.12 *Invalidity.* In the event any one or more of the provisions contained in this Agreement or in any other instrument referred to herein, shall, for any reason, be held to be invalid, illegal or unenforceable in any respect, such invalidity, illegality or unenforceability shall not affect any other provision of this Agreement or any other such instrument.

12.13 *Headings.* The headings of the several Sections herein are inserted for convenience of reference only and are not intended to be a part of or to affect the meaning or interpretation of this Agreement.

12.14 *Confidentiality of Information.* All information obtained by either party from the other pursuant to this Agreement shall be and remain confidential. Superior and Austral hereby agree that in the event the transactions contemplated herein are not consummated, each party will keep in strictest confidence all information (other than information which is known to be a matter of public knowledge) regarding the other party which may be acquired in connection with the matters contemplated herein.

12.15 *Expenses of This Agreement.* Except as otherwise provided herein, each party shall be solely responsible for all expenses incurred by it in connection with this transaction (including but not limited to fees and expenses of its own counsel and accountants) and shall not be entitled to any reimbursement therefor from the other party hereto.

12.16 *Bulk Sales.*   Subject to the provisions of Section 1 i, Superior waives compliance by Austral with any applicable bulk sales or similar law.

12.17 *Voting of Austral Stock.*   Superior agrees to vote or cause to be voted at the Austral Stockholders' Meeting all shares of Austral common stock which it beneficially owns in favor of the adoption of the Plan.

12.18 *Use of Austral Names.*   Superior agrees that, as soon as practicable after the Closing, it will remove or cause to be removed the names and marks "Austral", "Austral Oil Company Incorporated" and all variations and derivatives thereof and logos relating thereto from the Properties and will not thereafter make any use whatsoever of such names, marks and logos in connection with its business. The foregoing notwithstanding, Superior shall have the limited right to use the corporate and business name "Austral Petroleum Gas Corporation" and the abbreviation "APG" pursuant to a license substantially in the form of Exhibit 12.18.

IN WITNESS WHEREOF, the parties hereto have caused this Agreement to be duly executed on their respective behalves, by their respective officers, thereunto duly authorized, such officers' signatures having been duly attested, in multiple originals, all as of the day and year first above written.

THE SUPERIOR OIL COMPANY

By   CHARLES L. BARNEY
Vice President

ATTEST:

ALLAN C. DURHAM
Secretary

AUSTRAL OIL COMPANY INCORPORATED

By   PAUL R. COLE
President

ATTEST:

K. R. SCHNEIDER
Secretary

The undersigned attorneys for Austral Oil Company Incorporated and The Superior Oil Company, respectively, execute this Agreement for the limited purpose of acknowledging that on their advice their respective clients agreed to the provisions contained in Sections 3, 4 and 10 of this Agreement, which require that certain disputes be resolved by Arthur Young & Company or an independent petroleum engineering firm, and for the purpose of complying with the Texas General Arbitration Act, as amended.

Vinson & Elkins
Attorneys for Austral Oil
Company Incorporated

Bracewell & Patterson
Attorneys for The Superior
Oil Company

STATE OF TEXAS }
COUNTY OF HARRIS }

On this 10th day of March, 1978, before me appeared PAUL R. COLE, to me personally known, who being by me duly sworn, did say that he is the President of AUSTRAL OIL COMPANY INCORPORATED and that said instrument was signed in behalf of said corporation by authority of its Board of Directors and said PAUL R. COLE acknowledged said instrument to be the free act and deed of said corporation.

SHELIA BRASHIER
Notary Public in and for Harris County, Texas

My Commission Expires:
June 30, 1978

STATE OF TEXAS }
COUNTY OF HARRIS }

On this 10th day of March, 1978, before me appeared CHARLES L. BARNEY, to me personally known, who, being by me duly sworn, did say that he is a Vice President of THE SUPERIOR OIL COMPANY and that said instrument was signed in behalf of said corporation by authority of its Board of Directors and said CHARLES L. BARNEY acknowledged said instrument to be the free act and deed of said corporation.

SHELIA BRASHIER
Notary Public in and for Harris County, Texas

My Commission Expires:
June 30, 1978

APPENDIX E

Liquidating Trust Agreement for Barber Oil Corporation

BARBER OIL CORPORATION LIQUIDATING TRUST AGREEMENT

AGREEMENT AND DECLARATION OF TRUST by and between Barber Oil Corporation, a corporation in dissolution under the laws of the state of Delaware, hereinafter called "Barber", and

hereinafter collectively called the Trustees.

WHEREAS: On October 2, 1980, the Board of Directors of Barber voted to submit to the stockholders of Barber a Plan of Complete Liquidation and Dissolution (the "Plan"). The Plan was adopted by the stockholders of Barber at a meeting thereof held on December 29, 1980. The Plan provides for the creation of this liquidating trust.

Now, THEREFORE, in consideration of the premises and other valuable consideration, the receipt and sufficiency of which are hereby acknowledged, Barber hereby grants, releases, assigns, transfers, conveys and delivers unto the Trustees all of Barber's right, title and interest in and to all assets (tangible or intangible, known or unknown, whether personal property, real property or mixed) it owns, holds, or otherwise possesses any interest in, together with the appurtenances and all the estate and rights of Barber in and to such assets, except for those assets that the Board of Directors of Barber has determined should be distributed directly to stockholders of Barber contemporaneously with the distribution to such stockholders of their interests in this trust, in trust for the uses and purposes stated hereinabove, subject to the terms and provisions set out below, and the Trustees hereby accept such assets and such Trust, subject to the same terms and provisions; to wit:

ARTICLE 1.

NAME AND DEFINITIONS

1.1 *Name.* This trust shall be known as the Barber Oil Corporation Liquidating Trust.

1.2 *Certain Terms Defined.* For all purposes of this instrument, unless the context otherwise requires:

(a) *Agreement or Agreement of Trust* shall mean this instrument as originally executed or as it may from time to time be amended pursuant to the terms hereof.

(b) *Barber* shall mean Barber Oil Corporation, a corporation organized under the laws of the state of Delaware.

(c) *Beneficiaries* shall mean stockholders of Barber determined as of the Record Date and their legal representatives, heirs or successors.

(d) *Beneficial Interest* shall mean (i) at the commencement of this Agreement, the proportionate share of each beneficiary in the Trust Estate determined by the ratio of the number of issued and outstanding shares of Common Stock of Barber each beneficiary held on the Record Date to the number of issued and outstanding shares of such stock held by all beneficiaries on the Record Date, and (ii) thereafter, as each beneficiary's interest in the Trust Estate shall appear in the records of the Trustees.

(e) *Record Date* shall mean the date on which the holders of outstanding shares of Common Stock of Barber were determined by the Board of Directors of Barber to be entitled to the final liquidating distribution under the Plan.

(f) *Stockholders* shall mean the holders of record of the shares of the outstanding Common Stock of Barber on the Record Date.

(g) *Trust Estate* shall mean all the property held from time to time by the Trustees under this Agreement of Trust.

Exhibit 1 to Appendix I

(h) *Trust Assets* shall mean all dividends, rents, royalties, income, proceeds, and other receipts of or from the Trust Estate, including but not limited to (i) dividends and other cash distributions from any corporation, all or a portion of the outstanding stock of which is part of the Trust Estate, (ii) compensation for any part of the Trust Estate taken by eminent domain, (iii) proceeds (whether cash or securities) of sale of any part of the Trust Estate, (iv) proceeds of insurance upon any part of the Trust Estate, and (v) interest earned on any moneys or securities held by the Trustees under this Agreement of Trust.

(i) *Trustees* shall mean the original Trustees and their successors.

1.3 *Meaning of Other Terms.* Except where the context otherwise requires, words importing the masculine gender include the feminine and the neuter, if appropriate, words importing the singular number shall include the plural number and vice versa, and words importing persons shall include firms, associations, and corporations. All references herein to Articles, Sections, and other subdivisions refer to the corresponding Articles, Sections, and other subdivisions of this instrument; and the words herein, hereof, hereby, hereunder, and words of similar import, refer to this instrument as a whole and not to any particular Article, Section, or subdivision of the Agreement.

ARTICLE II.

NATURE OF TRANSFER

2.1 *Purpose of Trust.* The sole purpose of this Trust is to liquidate the Trust Estate in a manner calculated to conserve and protect the value of the Trust Estate, and to collect and distribute the Trust Estate and Trust Assets to the beneficiaries in as prompt and orderly a fashion as possible after the payment of, or provision for, expenses and liabilities.

2.2 *No Reversion to Barber.* In no event shall any part of the Trust Estate revert to or be distributed to Barber.

2.3 *Instruments of Further Assurance.* Barber and such persons as shall have the right and power after the dissolution of Barber will, upon reasonable request of the Trustees, execute, acknowledge, and deliver such further instruments and do such further acts as may be necessary or proper to effectively carry out the purposes of this Agreement, to transfer any property intended to be covered hereby, and to vest in the Trustees, their successors and assigns, the estate, powers, instruments or funds in trust hereunder.

2.4 *Payment of Barber Liabilities.* The Trustees hereby assume all the liabilities and claims (including unascertained or contingent liabilities and expenses) of Barber. With respect to claims by officers, directors or other persons for indemnification under Barber's Bylaws, the Trustees may engage independent legal counsel acceptable to them to render a written opinion as to whether the applicable standard of conduct set forth in Barber's Bylaws has been met. Should any liability be asserted against the Trustees as the transferees of the Trust Estate or as a result of the assumption made in this paragraph the Trustees may use such part of the Trust Estate as may be necessary in contesting any such liability or in payment thereof.

ARTICLE III.

BENEFICIARIES

3.1 *Beneficial Interests.* The beneficial interest of each beneficiary shall be determined in accordance with a certified copy of Barber's stockholder list as of the Record Date. Barber will deliver such a certified copy of its stockholder list to the Trustees within a reasonable time after such date. For ease of administration, the Trustees may, if they so elect, express the beneficial interest of each beneficiary in terms of units (when not specifically required to do so by any provision herein).

Exhibit I to Appendix I

3.1.1 If any conflicting claims or demands are made or asserted to any shares of Barber Common Stock, or to any interest of any beneficiary herein, or if there should be any disagreement between the transferees, assignees, heirs, representatives or legatees succeeding to all or a part of the interest of any beneficiary resulting in adverse claims or demands being made in connection with such interest, then, in any of such events, the Trustees shall be entitled, at their sole election, to refuse to comply with any such conflicting claims or demands. In so refusing, the Trustees may elect to make no payment or distribution to the interest represented by the Common Stock or units of Beneficial Interest involved, or any part thereof, and in so doing the Trustees shall not be or become liable to any of such parties for their failure or refusal to comply with any of such conflicting claims or demands, nor shall the Trustees be liable for interest on any funds which it may so withhold. The Trustees shall be entitled to refrain and refuse to act until (i) the rights of the adverse claimants have been adjudicated by a final judgment of a court of competent jurisdiction, (ii) all differences have been adjusted by valid written agreement between all of such parties, and the Trustees shall have been furnished with an executed counterpart of such agreement, or (iii) there is furnished to the Trustees a surety bond or other security satisfactory to the Trustees, as they shall deem appropriate, to fully indemnify them as between all conflicting claims or demands.

3.1.2 All liquidating distributions and other payments due any stockholder who has failed to surrender his certificates of Common Stock shall be retained by the Trustees for his benefit (a) until (i) his certificates of stock are surrendered or (ii) he furnishes the Trustees with evidence satisfactory to them of the loss, theft, or destruction of such certificates of stock and a surety bond satisfactory to them, unlimited in amount if they shall so specify, or such other security or indemnity as may be required by them, in either of which event the Trustees shall release all liquidating distributions due such stockholder to him, or (b) until the applicable escheat laws cause the reversion of such distributions or payments to the state. If required by the Trustees, any such stockholder may also be required, as a condition precedent to the release of any liquidating distributions due him, to pay all reasonable costs, expenses and attorneys' fees incurred in connection with proof of his ownership and cancellation of his certificates of Barber stock.

3.1.3 In addition to the benefits of Section 3.1.2 of this Agreement any beneficiary whose certificates of Barber stock are cancelled subsequent to the transfer of assets to the Trustees shall be entitled to the benefits of this Agreement of Trust equally and ratably with all beneficiaries.

3.2 *Rights of Beneficiaries.* Each beneficiary shall be entitled to participation in the rights and benefits due to a beneficiary hereunder according to his beneficial interest. Each beneficiary shall take and hold the same subject to all the terms and provisions of this Agreement of Trust. The interest of the beneficiary is hereby declared and shall be in all respects personal property and upon the death of an individual beneficiary his interest shall pass to his legal representative and such death shall in no wise terminate or affect the validity of this Agreement. A beneficiary shall have no title to, right to, possession of, management of, or control of, the Trust Estate except as herein expressly provided. No widower, widow, heir, or devisee of any person who may be a beneficiary shall have any right of dower, homestead, or inheritance, or of partition, or of any other right, statutory or otherwise, in any property whatever forming a part of the Trust Estate, but the whole title to all the Trust Estate shall be vested in the Trustees and the sole interest of the beneficiaries shall be the rights and benefits given to such persons under the Agreement of Trust.

3.3 *No Transfer of Interests of Beneficiaries.* The interest of a beneficiary may not be transferred either by the beneficiary in person or by a duly authorized agent or attorney, or by the properly appointed legal representatives of the beneficiary, nor may a beneficiary have authority or power to sell, assign, transfer, encumber, or in any other manner anticipate or dispose of his interest in the trust; provided, however, that the interest of a beneficiary shall be transferable by will, intestate succession, or operation of law.

Exhibit 1 to Appendix 1

3.4 *Applicable Law.* As to matters affecting the title, ownership, transferability, or attachment of the interest of a beneficiary in the Trust, the laws from time to time in force in the state of Delaware shall govern.

3.5 *Trustees as Beneficiaries.* Each Trustee, either individually or in a representative or fiduciary capacity, may be a beneficiary to the same extent as if he were not a Trustee hereunder.

ARTICLE IV.

DURATION AND TERMINATION OF TRUST

4.1 *Duration.* The existence of this Trust shall terminate upon the distribution of all of the Trust Estate as provided in Section 5.5.

4.2 *Termination by Beneficiaries.* The Trust may be terminated at any time by the action of beneficiaries having in the aggregate a majority of the beneficial interests as evidenced in the manner provided in Article XII.

4.3 *Continuance of Trust for Winding Up.* After the termination of the Trust and for the purpose of liquidating and winding up the affairs of this Trust, the Trustees shall continue to act as such until their duties have been fully performed. Upon distribution of all of the Trust Estate, the Trustees shall retain the books, records, stockholder lists, Common Stock certificates and files which shall have been delivered to or created by the Trustees. At the Trustees' discretion, all of such records and documents may be destroyed at any time after three years from the distribution of all of the Trust Estate. Except as otherwise specifically provided herein, upon the distribution of all of the Trust Estate, the Trustees shall have no further duties or obligations hereunder except to account as provided in Section 5.6.

ARTICLE V.

ADMINISTRATION OF TRUST ESTATE

5.1 *Sale of Trust Estate.* The Trustees may, at such times as they may deem appropriate, transfer, assign, or otherwise dispose of all or any part of the Trust Estate as they deem appropriate at public auction or at private sale for cash or securities, or upon credit (either secured or unsecured as the Trustees shall determine).

5.2 *Collection of Trust Assets.* All Trust Assets shall be collected by the Trustees and held as a part of the Trust Estate. The Trustees shall hold the Trust Estate without provision for or the payment of any interest thereon to any beneficiary.

5.3 *Payment of Claims, Expenses and Liabilities.* The Trustees shall pay from the Trust Estate all claims, expenses, charges, liabilities, and obligations of the Trust Estate and all liabilities and obligations which the Trustees specifically assume and agree to pay pursuant to this Agreement of Trust and such transferee liabilities which the Trustees may be obligated to pay as transferees of the Trust Estate, including among the foregoing, and without limiting the generality of the foregoing, interest, taxes, assessments, and public charges of every kind and nature and the costs, charges, and expenses connected with or growing out of the execution or administration of this Trust and such other payments and disbursements as are provided in this Agreement or which may be determined to be a proper charge against the Trust Estate by the Trustees. The Trustees may, in their discretion, make provisions by reserve or otherwise out of the Trust Assets or the Trust Estate, for such amount as the Trustees in good faith may determine to be necessary to meet present or future claims and liabilities of the Trust, whether fixed or contingent.

Exhibit 1 to Appendix 1

5.4   Interim Distributions. At such times as may be determined by them, the Trustees shall distribute, or cause to be distributed, to the beneficiaries of record on the close of business on such record date as the Trustees may determine, in proportion to their respective Beneficial Interests, such cash or non-cash property comprising a portion of the Trust Estate as the Trustees may in their sole discretion determine may be distributed without detriment to the conservation and protection of the value of the remaining Trust Estate. The Trustees shall not retain in the Trust Estate cash in excess of a reasonable amount necessary to meet present or future claims or liabilities of the Trust Estate, whether fixed or contingent.

5.5   Final Distribution. If the Trustees determine that all claims, debts, liabilities, and obligations of the Trust have been paid or discharged, or if the existence of the Trust shall terminate pursuant to Section 4.2, the Trustees shall, as expeditiously as is consistent with the conservation and protection of the Trust Estate, distribute the Trust Estate to the beneficiaries of record on the close of business on such record date as the Trustees may determine, in proportion to their beneficial interests therein; provided, however, that if the Trust is terminated pursuant to Section 4.2, the Trust Estate shall be distributed subject to any and all remaining liabilities and claims not matured at the date of such distribution. The Trustees shall make disposition of all liquidating distributions and other payments due any Stockholders who have not been located or who have not surrendered their certificates of Common Stock for cancellation pursuant to Section 3.1 in accordance with Delaware law.

5.6   Reports to Beneficiaries. As soon as practicable after the end of each fiscal year of the Trust and after termination of the Trust, the Trustees shall submit a written report and account to the beneficiaries showing (i) the assets and liabilities of the Trust at the end of such fiscal year or upon termination and the receipts and disbursements of the Trustees for such fiscal year or period, certified by independent public accountants, (ii) any changes in the Trust Estate which they have not previously reported, and (iii) any action taken by the Trustees in the performance of their duties under this Agreement of Trust which they have not previously reported and which, in their opinion, materially affects the Trust Estate. The Trustees may submit similar reports for such interim periods during the fiscal year as they deem advisable. The approval by beneficiaries having an aggregate Beneficial Interest of more than 50% of any report or account shall, as to all matters and transactions disclosed therein, be final and binding upon all persons, whether in being or not, who may then or thereafter become interested in the Trust Estate. The fiscal year of the Trust shall end on September 30 of each year unless the Trustees deem it advisable to establish some other date as the date on which the fiscal year of the Trust shall end.

5.7   Federal Income Tax Information. As soon as practicable after the close of each fiscal year, the Trustees shall mail to each beneficiary of record at the close of such year, a statement showing on a unit basis the dates and amounts of all distributions made by the Trustees, depletion and depreciation allowances, if any, and such other information as is reasonably available to the Trustees which may be helpful in determining the amount of taxable income from the Trust that such beneficiary should include in his Federal income tax return in respect of such year. In addition, after receipt of a request in good faith, or in their discretion without such request, the Trustees may furnish to any person who has been a beneficiary at any time during such year a statement containing such further information as is reasonably available to the Trustees which may be helpful in determining the amount of taxable income which such person should include in his Federal income tax return.

ARTICLE VI.

POWERS OF AND LIMITATIONS ON THE TRUSTEES

6.1   Limitations on Trustees. The Trustees shall not at any time, on behalf of the Trust or beneficiaries, enter into or engage in any business, and no part of the Trust Estate or the Trust Assets shall be used or disposed of by the Trustees in furtherance of any business. This limitation shall apply irrespective of whether the conduct of any such business activities is deemed by the Trustees to be convenient, desirable, necessary or proper for the conservation and protection of the Trust Estate. The Trustees shall

Exhibit 1 to Appendix 1

not invest any of the funds held in the Trust Estate, except that the Trustees may invest any portion of the Trust Estate in certificates of deposit of domestic banks having in excess of $10,000,000 in capital and surplus, savings accounts or certificates of deposit issued by any savings institution insured by the Federal Savings and Loan Insurance Corporation, and marketable direct obligations of, or guaranteed as to principal and interest by, the United States Government or any agency thereof. The Trustees shall be restricted to the holding and collection of the Trust Assets and the payment and distribution thereof for the purposes set forth in this Agreement and to the conservation and protection of the Trust Estate and the administration thereof in accordance with the provisions of this Agreement. In no event shall the Trustees receive any property, make any distribution, incur, satisfy or discharge any obligation, claim, liability or expense or otherwise take any action which is inconsistent with a complete liquidation of Barber as that term is used in Sections 337 and 331 of the Internal Revenue Code of 1954 and interpreted by regulations promulgated thereunder, and rulings, decisions, and determinations of the Internal Revenue Service and courts of competent jurisdiction.

6.2 *Specific Powers of Trustees.* Subject to the provisions of Section 6.1, the Trustees shall have the following specific powers in addition to any powers conferred upon them by any other Section or provision of this Agreement of Trust; provided, however, that enumeration of the following powers shall not be considered in any way to limit or control the power of the Trustees to act as specifically authorized by any other Section or provision of this Agreement and to act in such a manner as the Trustees may deem necessary or appropriate to conserve and protect the Trust Estate or to confer on the beneficiaries the benefits intended to be conferred upon them by this Agreement:

(a) To determine the terms on which assets comprising the Trust Estate should be sold or otherwise disposed of;

(b) To collect and receive any and all money and other property of whatsoever kind or nature due to or owing or belonging to the trust and to give full discharge and acquittance therefor;

(c) Pending sale or other disposition or distribution, to retain all or any assets constituting part of the Trust Estate regardless of whether or not such assets are, or may become, underproductive, unproductive or a wasting asset, or whether such assets, if considered to be investments, might be considered to be speculative or extrahazardous. The Trustees shall not be under any duty to reinvest such part of the Trust Estate as may be in cash, or as may be converted into cash, nor shall the Trustees be chargeable with interest thereon except to the extent that interest may be paid to the trust on such cash amounts;

(d) To retain and set aside such funds out of the Trust Estate as the Trustees shall deem necessary or expedient to pay, or provide for the payment of (i) unpaid claims, liabilities, debts or obligations of the trust or Barber, (ii) contingencies, and (iii) the expenses of administering the Trust Estate.

(e) To do and perform any acts or things necessary or appropriate for the conservation and protection of the Trust Estate, including acts or things necessary or appropriate to maintain assets held by the Trustees pending sale or other disposition thereof or distribution thereof to the beneficiaries, and in connection therewith to employ such agents and to confer upon them such authority as the Trustees may deem expedient, and to pay reasonable compensation therefor;

(f) To cause any investments of Trust Assets to be registered and held in the name of any one or more of their names or in the names of a nominee or nominees without increase or decrease of liability with respect thereto;

(g) To institute or defend actions or declaratory judgments or other actions and to take such other action, in the name of the trust or of Barber if otherwise required, as the Trustees may deem necessary or desirable to enforce any instruments, contracts, agreements, or causes of action relating to or forming a part of the Trust Estate.

Exhibit 1 to Appendix I

(h) To cancel, terminate, or amend any instruments, contracts, or agreements relating to or forming a part of the Trust Estate, and to execute new instruments, contracts, or agreements, notwithstanding that the terms of any such instruments, contracts, or agreements may extend beyond the terms of this trust, provided that no such new instrument, contract, or agreement shall permit the Trustees to engage in any activity prohibited by Section 6.1;

(i) To vote by proxy or otherwise and with full power of substitution all shares of stock and all securities held by the Trustees hereunder and to exercise every power, election, discretion, option and subscription right and give every notice, make every demand, and to do every act and thing in respect to any shares of stock or other securities held by the Trustees which the Trustees might or could do if they were the absolute owners thereof;

(j) To undertake or join in any merger, plan of reorganization, consolidation, liquidation, dissolution or readjustment of any corporation, any of whose shares of stock or other securities, obligations, or properties may at any time constitute a part of the Trust Estate, and to accept the substituted shares of stock, bonds, securities, obligations and properties and to hold the same in trust in accordance with the provisions hereof;

(k) In connection with the sale or other disposition or distribution of any securities held by the Trustees, to comply with the applicable Federal and state securities laws, and to enter into agreements relating to sale or other disposition or distribution thereof;

(l) To contract for and to borrow money in such amounts as the Trustees deem advisable for any trust purpose (including, but without limitation, protecting or conserving any portion of the Trust Estate and making any payment of income or principal) and, in connection therewith, to draw, make, accept, endorse, execute, issue and deliver promissory notes, drafts and other negotiable or transferable instruments and evidence of indebtedness and all renewals or extensions of same;

(m) To authorize transactions between corporations or other entities held by the Trustees as part of the Trust Estate;

(n) In the event any of the property which is or may become a part of the Trust Estate is situated in any state or other jurisdiction in which any Trustee is not qualified to act as Trustee, to nominate and appoint an individual or corporate trustee qualified to act in such state or other jurisdiction in connection with the property situated in that state or other jurisdiction as a trustee of such property and require from such trustee such security as may be designated by the Trustees. The trustee so appointed shall have all the rights, powers, privileges and duties and shall be subject to the conditions and limitations of this trust, except as modified or limited by the Trustees and except where the same may be modified by the laws of such state or other jurisdiction (in which case, the laws of the state or other jurisdiction in which such trustee is acting shall prevail to the extent necessary). Such trustee shall be answerable to the Trustees here appointed for all monies, assets and other property which may be received by it in connection with the administration of such property. The Trustees hereunder may remove such trustee, with or without cause, and appoint a successor trustee at any time by the execution by the Trustees of a written instrument declaring such trustee removed from office, and specifying the effective date and time of removal;

(o) To grant or consent to licenses, easements, and consents for roads, rights-of-way, power lines, telephone lines, pipe lines, boundary line agreements, and similar uses and to grant other usage rights, on or with respect to the Trust Estate, whether or not the term thereof may extend beyond the duration of this trust;

(p) To perform any act authorized, permitted, or required under any instrument, contract, agreement, or cause of action relating to or forming a part of the Trust Estate whether in the nature of an approval, consent, demand, or notice thereunder or otherwise, unless such act would require the consent of the beneficiaries in accordance with the express provisions of this Agreement.

Exhibit I to Appendix I

ARTICLE VII

CONCERNING THE TRUSTEES

7.1 *Generally*. The Trustees accept and undertake to discharge the trusts created by this Agreement, upon the terms and conditions thereof. The Trustees shall exercise such of the rights and powers vested in them by this Agreement, and use the same degree of care and skill in their exercise as a prudent man would exercise or use under the circumstances in the conduct of his own affairs. No provision of this Agreement shall be construed to relieve the Trustees from liability for their own negligent action, their own negligent failure to act, or their own wilful misconduct, except that:

(a) No Trustee shall be responsible for the acts or omissions of any other Trustee if done or omitted without his knowledge or consent unless it shall be proved that such Trustee was negligent in ascertaining the pertinent facts, and no successor Trustee shall be in any way responsible for the acts or omissions of any Trustees in office prior to the date on which he becomes a Trustee.

(b) No Trustee shall be liable except for the performance of such duties and obligations as are specifically set forth in this Agreement, and no implied covenants or obligations shall be read into this Agreement against the Trustees.

(c) In the absence of bad faith on the part of the Trustees, the Trustees may conclusively rely, as to the truth of the statements and the correctness of the opinions expressed therein, upon any certificates or opinions furnished to the Trustees and conforming to the requirements of this Agreement; but in the case of any such certificates or opinions which are specifically required to be furnished to the Trustees by any provision hereof, the Trustees shall be under a duty to examine the same to determine whether or not they conform to the requirements of this Agreement.

(d) No Trustee shall be liable for any error of judgment made in good faith.

(e) No Trustee shall be liable with respect to any action taken or omitted to be taken by them in good faith in accordance with the direction of beneficiaries having an aggregate beneficial interest of more than 50% relating to the time, method, and place of conducting any proceeding for any remedy available to the Trustees, or exercising any trust or power conferred upon the Trustees under this Agreement.

7.2 *Reliance by Trustees*. Except as otherwise provided in Section 7.1:

(a) The Trustees may rely and shall be protected in acting upon any resolution, certificate, statement, instrument, opinion, report, notice, request, consent, order, or other paper or document believed by them to be genuine and to have been signed or presented by the proper party or parties.

(b) The Trustees may consult with legal counsel to be selected by them, and the Trustees shall not be liable for any action taken or suffered by them in accordance with the advice of such counsel.

(c) Persons dealing with Trustees shall look only to the Trust Estate to satisfy any liability incurred by the Trustees to such person in carrying out the terms of this trust, and the Trustees shall have no personal or individual obligation to satisfy any such liability.

7.3 *Indemnification of Trustees*. Each Trustee shall be indemnified by and receive reimbursement from the Trust Estate against and from any and all loss, liability or damage which such Trustee may incur or sustain, in good faith and without gross negligence, in the exercise and performance of any of the powers and duties of such Trustee under this Agreement. The Trustees may purchase with assets of the Trust Estate, such insurance as they feel, in the exercise of their discretion, adequately insures that each Trustee shall be indemnified against any such loss, liability or damage pursuant to this Section.

Exhibit 1 to Appendix I

ARTICLE VIII.

PROTECTION OF PERSONS DEALING WITH THE TRUSTEES

8.1 *Action by Trustees.* All action required or permitted to be taken by the Trustees, in their capacity as Trustees, shall be taken (i) at a meeting at which a quorum is present, having been duly called by one or more of the Trustees on at least three days' prior written or telegraphic notice to all of the Trustees then serving, or (ii) without a meeting, by a written vote. resolution, or other writing signed by all the Trustees then serving. Except where this Agreement otherwise provides, all action taken at such a meeting shall be by vote or resolution of a majority of such of the Trustees as are present and shall have the same force and effect as if taken by all the Trustees. A majority of the Trustees then serving shall constitute a quorum.

8.2 *Reliance on Statement by Trustees.* Any person dealing with the Trustees shall be fully protected in relying upon the Trustees' certificate signed by any one or more of the Trustees that they have authority to take any action under this trust. Any person dealing with the Trustees shall be fully protected in relying upon the Trustees' certificate setting forth the facts concerning the calling of any meeting of the beneficiaries, the giving of notice thereof, and the action taken at such meeting, including the aggregate beneficial interest of beneficiaries taking such action.

8.3 *Application of Money Paid or Transferred to Trustees.* No person dealing with the Trustees shall be required to follow the application by the Trustees of any money or property which may be paid or transferred to the Trustees.

ARTICLE IX.

COMPENSATION OF TRUSTEES

9.1 *Amount of Compensation.* In lieu of commissions or other compensation fixed by law for trustees, each Trustee shall receive as compensation for services as Trustee hereunder and as additional compensation from the cash proceeds of the sale of any part of the Trust Estate while he is serving as Trustee, such compensation as shall be first determined by the Board of Directors of Barber at the time this Agreement is entered into, or as may subsequently be approved by beneficiaries having an aggregate beneficial interest of more than 50%.

9.2 *Dates of Payment.* The compensation payable to each Trustee pursuant to the provisions of Section 9.1 shall be paid quarterly or at such other times as the Trustees may determine.

9.3 *Expenses.* Each Trustee shall be reimbursed from the Trust Estate for all expenses reasonably incurred by him in the performance of his duties in accordance with this Agreement.

ARTICLE X.

TRUSTEES AND SUCCESSOR TRUSTEES

10.1 *Number of Trustees.* Subject to the provisions of Section 10.3 relating to the period pending the appointment of a successor Trustee. there shall always be three Trustees of this trust, each of whom shall be a citizen and resident of the United States.

If any corporate Trustee shall ever change its name, or shall reorganize or reincorporate, or shall merge with or into or consolidate with any other bank or trust company, such corporate Trustee shall be deemed to be a continuing entity and shall continue to act as a Trustee hereunder with the same liabilities, duties, powers, titles, discretions and privileges as are herein specified for a Trustee.

Exhibit I to Appendix I

10.2 *Resignation and Removal.* Any Trustee may resign and be discharged from the trusts hereby created by giving written notice thereof to the remaining Trustees and by mailing such notice to the beneficiaries at their respective addresses as they appear in the records of the Trustees. Such resignation shall become effective on the day specified in such notice or upon the appointment of such Trustee's successor and such successor's acceptance of such appointment, whichever is earlier. Any Trustee may be removed at any time, with or without cause, by beneficiaries having in the aggregate a majority of the beneficial interests.

10.3 *Appointment of Successor.* Should at any time a Trustee resign or be removed, or die or become incapable of action, or be adjudged a bankrupt or insolvent, a vacancy shall be deemed to exist and a successor shall be appointed by the remaining Trustees. If such vacancy is not filled by the remaining Trustees within 30 days, the beneficiaries may, pursuant to Article XIII hereof, call a meeting to appoint a successor Trustee by majority in interest. Pending the appointment of a successor Trustee, the remaining Trustees then serving may take any action in the manner set forth in Section 8.1.

10.4 *Acceptance of Appointment by Successor Trustee.* Any successor Trustee appointed hereunder shall execute an instrument accepting such appointment hereunder and shall deliver one counterpart thereof each to the other Trustees and, in case of a resignation, to the retiring Trustee. Thereupon such successor Trustee shall, without any further act, become vested with all the estates, properties, rights, powers, trusts, and duties of his or its predecessor in the trust hereunder with like effect as if originally named therein; but the retiring Trustee shall nevertheless, when requested in writing by the successor Trustee or by the remaining Trustees, execute and deliver an instrument or instruments conveying and transferring to such successor Trustee upon the trust herein expressed, all the estates, properties, rights, powers and trusts of such retiring Trustee, and shall duly assign, transfer, and deliver to such successor Trustee all property and money held by him hereunder.

10.5 *Bonds.* Unless required by the Board of Directors of Barber prior to the transfer of assets to the Trustees, or unless a bond is required by law, no bond shall be required of any original Trustee hereunder. Unless required by a majority vote of the Trustees prior to a successor Trustee's acceptance of an appointment as such pursuant to Section 10.4, or unless a bond is required by law, no bond shall be required of any successor Trustee hereunder. If a bond is required by law, no surety or security with respect to such bond shall be required unless required by law or unless required by the Board of Directors of Barber (in the case of an original Trustee) or the Trustees (in the case of a successor Trustee). If a bond is required, the Board of Directors of Barber or the Trustees, as the case may be, shall determine whether, and to what extent, a surety or security with respect to such bond shall be required.

ARTICLE XI.

CONCERNING THE BENEFICIARIES

11.1 *Evidence of Action by Beneficiaries.* Whenever in this Agreement it is provided that the beneficiaries may take any action (including the making of any demand or request, the giving of any notice, consent, or waiver, the removal of a Trustee, the appointment of a successor Trustee, or the taking of any other action), the fact that at the time of taking any such action such holders have joined therein may be evidenced (i) by any instrument or any number of instruments of similar tenor executed by beneficiaries in person or by agent or attorney appointed in writing, or (ii) by the record of the beneficiaries voting in favor thereof at any meeting of beneficiaries duly called and held in accordance with the provisions of Article XII.

11.2 *Limitation on Suits by Beneficiaries.* No beneficiary shall have any right by virtue of any provision of this Agreement to institute any action or proceeding at law or in equity against any party other than the Trustees upon or under or with respect to the Trust Estate or the agreements relating to or forming part of the Trust Estate, and the beneficiaries do hereby waive any such right, unless beneficiaries having an aggregate beneficial interest of 25% shall have made written request upon the Trustees to

Exhibit 1 to Appendix 1

institute such action or proceeding in their own names as Trustees hereunder and shall have offered to the Trustees reasonable indemnity against the costs and expenses to be incurred therein or thereby, and the Trustees for 30 days after their receipt of such notice, request, and offer of indemnity shall have failed to institute any such action or proceeding.

11.3 *Requirement of Undertaking.* The Trustees may request any court to require, and any court may in its discretion require, in any suit for the enforcement of any right or remedy under this Agreement, or in any suit against the Trustees for any action taken or omitted by them as Trustees, the filing by any party litigant in such suit of an undertaking to pay the costs of such suit, and such court may in its discretion assess reasonable costs, including reasonable attorneys' fees, against any party litigant in such suit, having due regard to the merits and good faith of the claims or defenses made by such party litigant; provided, that the provisions of this Section shall not apply to any suit by the Trustees, and such undertaking shall not be requested by the Trustees or otherwise required in any suit by any beneficiary or group of beneficiaries having an aggregate beneficial interest of more than 5%.

ARTICLE XII.

MEETING OF BENEFICIARIES

12.1 *Purpose of Meetings.* A meeting of the beneficiaries may be called at any time and from time to time pursuant to the provisions of this Article for the purposes of taking any action which the terms of this Agreement permit a beneficiary having a specified aggregate beneficial interest to take either acting alone or with the Trustees.

12.2 *Meeting Called by Trustees.* The Trustees may at any time call a meeting of the beneficiaries to be held at such time and at such place within the state of Delaware (or elsewhere if so determined by a majority of the Trustees) as the Trustees shall determine. Written notice of every meeting of the beneficiaries shall be given by the Trustees (except as provided in Section 12.3), which written notice will set forth the time and place of such meeting and in general terms the action proposed to be taken at such meeting, and shall be mailed not more than 60 nor less than 10 days before such meeting is to be held to all of the beneficiaries of record not more than 60 days before the date of such meeting. The notice shall be directed to the beneficiaries at their respective addresses as they appear in the records of the Trustees.

12.3 *Meeting Called on Request of Beneficiaries.* Within 30 days after written request to the Trustees by beneficiaries having an aggregate Beneficial Interest of 25% to call a meeting of all the beneficiaries, which written request shall specify in reasonable detail the action proposed to be taken, the Trustees shall proceed under the provisions of Section 12.2 to call a meeting of the beneficiaries, and if the Trustees fail to call such meeting within such 30-day period then such meeting may be called by beneficiaries having an aggregate Beneficial Interest of 25% or their designated representative.

12.4 *Persons Entitled to Vote at Meeting of Beneficiaries.* Each beneficiary of record on a record date determined by the Trustees shall be entitled to vote at a meeting of the beneficiaries either in person or by his proxy duly authorized in writing. The signature of the beneficiary on such written authorization need not be witnessed or notarized.

12.5 *Quorum.* At any meeting of beneficiaries, the presence of beneficiaries having an aggregate beneficial interest sufficient to take action on any matter for the transaction of which such meeting was called shall be necessary to constitute a quorum; but if less than a quorum be present, beneficiaries having an aggregate Beneficial Interest of more than 50% of the aggregate Beneficial Interest of all beneficiaries represented at the meeting may adjourn such meeting with the same effect and for all intents and purposes as though a quorum had been present.

12.6 *Adjournment of Meeting.* Any meeting of beneficiaries may be adjourned from time to time and a meeting may be held at such adjourned time and place without further notice.

Exhibit 1 to Appendix 1

12.7 *Conduct of Meetings.* The Trustees shall appoint the Chairman and the Secretary of the meeting. The vote upon any resolution submitted to any meeting of beneficiaries shall be by written ballot. Two Inspectors of Votes, appointed by the Chairman of the meeting, shall count all votes cast at the meeting for or against any resolution and shall make and file with the Secretary of the meeting their verified written report.

12.8 *Record of Meeting.* A record of the proceedings of each meeting of beneficiaries shall be prepared by the Secretary of the meeting. The record shall be signed and verified by the Secretary of the meeting and shall be delivered to the Trustees to be preserved by them. Any record so signed and verified shall be conclusive evidence of all the matters therein stated.

ARTICLE XIII.

AMENDMENTS

13.1 *Consent of Beneficiaries.* At the direction or with the consent (evidenced in the manner provided in Section 11.1) of beneficiaries having in the aggregate a majority of the beneficial interests, the Trustees shall promptly make and execute a declaration amending this Agreement for the purpose of adding any provisions to or changing in any manner or eliminating any of the provisions of this Agreement or amendments hereto, provided, however, that no such amendment shall permit the Trustees hereunder to engage in any activity prohibited by Section 6.1 or affect the beneficiaries' rights to receive their pro rata shares of any distributions under this Agreement.

13.2 *Notice and Effect of Amendment.* Promptly after the execution by the Trustees of any such declaration of amendment, the Trustees shall give notice of the substance of such amendment to the beneficiaries or, in lieu thereof, the Trustees may send a copy of the amendment to each beneficiary. Upon the execution of any such declaration of amendment by the Trustees, this Agreement shall be deemed to be modified and amended in accordance therewith and the respective rights, limitations of rights, obligations, duties, and immunities of the Trustees and the beneficiaries under this Agreement shall thereafter be determined, exercised, and enforced hereunder subject in all respects to such modification and amendment, and all the terms and conditions of any such amendment shall be thereby deemed to be part of the terms and conditions of this Agreement for any and all purposes.

ARTICLE XIV.

MISCELLANEOUS PROVISIONS

14.1 *Filing Documents.* This Agreement shall be filed or recorded in the office of the Secretary of State of the State of Delaware, and in such other office or offices as the Trustees may determine to be necessary or desirable. A copy of this Agreement and all amendments thereof shall be filed in the office of each Trustee and shall be available at all times for inspection by any beneficiary or his duly authorized representative. The Trustees shall file or record any amendment of this Agreement in the same places where the original Agreement is filed or recorded. The Trustees shall file or record any instrument which relates to any change in the office of Trustee in the same places where the original Agreement is filed or recorded.

14.2 *Intention of Parties to Establish Trust.* This Agreement is not intended to create and shall not be interpreted as creating an association, partnership, or joint venture of any kind. It is intended as a trust to be governed and construed in all respects as a trust.

14.3 *Laws as to Construction.* This Agreement shall be governed by and construed in accordance with the laws of the state of Delaware.

Exhibit 1 to Appendix 1

14.4 *Separability*. In the event any provision of this Agreement or the application thereof to any person or circumstances shall be finally determined by a court of proper jurisdiction to be invalid or unenforceable to any extent, the remainder of this Agreement, or the application of such provision to persons or circumstances other than those as to which it is held invalid or unenforceable, shall not be affected thereby, and each provision of this Agreement shall be valid and enforced to the fullest extent permitted by law.

14.5 *Notices*. Any notice or other communication by the Trustees to any beneficiary shall be deemed to have been sufficiently given, for all purposes, if given by being deposited, postage prepaid, in a post office or letter box addressed to such person at his address as shown in the records of the Trustees.

14.6 *Counterparts*. This Agreement may be executed in any number of counterparts, each of which shall be an original, but such counterparts shall together constitute but one and the same instrument.

IN WITNESS WHEREOF, BARBER OIL CORPORATION has caused this Agreement to be signed and acknowledged by its Chairman of the Board and its corporate seal to be affixed hereto, and the same to be attested by its Secretary, and the Trustees herein have signed, sealed, and executed this Agreement, effective this day of   , 1981.

BARBER OIL CORPORATION

By:_____

Corporate Seal

ATTEST:

_____
        Secretary

_____

_____

_____
        Trustees

Exhibit 1 to Appendix 1

APPENDIX F

Opinions of Investment Bankers

Goldman, Sachs & Co. | 55 Broad Street | New York, New York 10004
Tel: 212-676-8000

Goldman
Sachs

May 10, 1976

Board of Directors
Pasco, Inc.
530 Fifth Avenue
New York, New York 10036

GENTLEMEN:

You have asked our opinion as to the fairness to Pasco, Inc. ("Pasco") of the financial terms as set forth in Sections 4 and 5 of an Agreement dated February 14, 1976 (the "Agreement"), attached as Appendix B to the Proxy Statement with respect to the Annual Meeting of Stockholders of Pasco scheduled to be held June 2, 1976, pursuant to which Sinclair Oil Corporation ("Sinclair"), owned 50% by Little America Refining Co. and 50% by Holding's Little America, would purchase certain assets of Pasco.

Goldman, Sachs & Co., as part of its investment banking business, is constantly engaged in the valuation of businesses and their securities in connection with mergers and acquisitions, negotiated underwritings, secondary distributions of listed and unlisted securities, private placements and valuations for estate, corporate and other purposes. In 1975 we advised Pasco in connection with the sale of certain of its assets to Amoco Production Company, a wholly-owned subsidiary of Standard Oil Company (Indiana); and have assisted Pasco in certain matters relating to the proposed transaction with Sinclair.

In the course of our review we have studied the Annual Reports and 10-K Reports of Pasco for four years ending December 31, 1975 and reports for certain interim periods and reviewed various documents in connection with the purchase by Pasco of substantially all of its assets from Atlantic Richfield Company in 1972, the Proxy Statements with respect to Pasco's Annual and Special Meetings of Stockholders in 1975 and a proof dated May 6, 1976 of the Proxy Statement with respect to Pasco's Annual Meeting of Stockholders for 1976 scheduled to be held June 2, 1976. In addition, we have discussed with officers of Pasco the past and current status of and outlook for Pasco's refining, marketing and pipeline businesses. We have also reviewed the financial terms of certain recent transactions which involved the sale or proposed sale of petroleum refining and/or marketing facilities.

Based upon the foregoing information and other factors we considered pertinent and our general knowledge of and experience in the valuation of businesses and their securities, it is our opinion that the financial terms of the proposed transaction with Sinclair, as set forth in Sections 4 and 5 of the Agreement, are fair and equitable to Pasco.

Very truly yours,

GOLDMAN, SACHS & CO.

New York | Boston | Chicago | Dallas | Los Angeles | Philadelphia | St. Louis | San Francisco | Detroit | Memphis

Oppenheimer & Co., Inc.

ONE NEW YORK PLAZA, NEW YORK CITY 10004, (212) 825-4000, CABLE ADDRESS: MOPENER NEW YORK

May 10, 1976

Board of Directors
Pasco, Inc.
530 Fifth Avenue
New York, New York 10036

GENTLEMEN:

You have advised us that Pasco, Inc. ("Pasco") proposes to sell its oil refinery in Wyoming, a wholly-owned pipeline subsidiary, a wholly-owned marketing subsidiary, inventories and certain other assets to Sinclair Oil Corporation ("Sinclair") for approximately $72,000,000, and you have asked our opinion as to the fairness of the financial terms of the proposed transaction to the public stockholders of Pasco.

The complete terms of the proposed transaction are set forth in the Agreement between the parties dated February 14, 1976, attached as Appendix B to a proof dated May 6, 1976 of the Proxy Statement with respect to the Annual Meeting of Stockholders of Pasco scheduled to be held June 2, 1976. With the exception of certain current assets (principally cash, securities and receivables), the assets to be sold to Sinclair ("Remaining Assets") constitute substantially all of Pasco's assets remaining after the sale of two gas processing plants and seven oil and gas fields to Amoco Production Company on December 30, 1975 (the "AMOCO Transaction").

At the time of the AMOCO Transaction we gave you our opinion that the plan of complete liquidation ("Plan") pursuant to Section 337 of the Internal Revenue Code of 1954 as well as the terms of the AMOCO Transaction were in the best interest of the public stockholders of Pasco. It is our understanding that as part of that Plan, the proposed transaction with Sinclair would not represent a taxable event for Pasco and the proceeds distributed to the public stockholders would be subject to capital gains tax treatment.

Together with Goldman, Sachs & Co., we were retained by Pasco to assist the company in its efforts to sell the Remaining Assets. In connection with this engagement, we analyzed the value of the Remaining Assets, prepared a memorandum describing those assets, and contacted and provided the memorandum to a number of prospective purchasers in order to identify any bona fide purchaser willing and able to offer the most favorable terms to Pasco.

Based on our analysis of the value of the Remaining Assets and on our contacts with prospective purchasers, we believe that the financial terms of the proposed transaction with Sinclair are fair to the public stockholders of Pasco.

Very truly yours,

OPPENHEIMER & CO., INC.

OPINION OF THE FIRST BOSTON CORPORATION

July 22, 1981

The Board of Directors
Great Basins Petroleum Co.
1011 Gateway West
Century City
Los Angeles, California 90067

Gentlemen:

You have asked us to advise you on the fairness to the shareholders of Great Basins Petroleum Co. ("Great Basins") of the financial terms of the proposed sale of three Canadian subsidiaries, Great Basins Petroleum Ltd., Great Basins Minerals Ltd. and Great Basins Oil & Gas Ltd. ("Canadian Petroleum Subsidiaries") to United Canso Oil & Gas Ltd. ("Canso"), as more fully described in the Proxy Statement of Great Basins dated July 22, 1981 (the "Great Basins Proxy Statement"), in connection with the special meeting of its stockholders scheduled for August 26. 1981.

On June 5, 1979, Great Basins' Board of Directors authorized management to explore the possibilities for the disposition by sale or merger of Great Basins' business and properties. First Boston was engaged by Great Basins on August 9, 1979 to act as its financial advisor in connection with the sale or disposition for cash or other consideration of Great Basins' Common Stock or assets. In that capacity, First Boston assisted Great Basins' management and legal advisors in the development of materials describing Great Basins and, on behalf of Great Basins, solicited proposals for the purchase of Great Basins which, on May 18, 1980, resulted in Phillips Petroleum Company ("Phillips") making a cash offer to acquire Great Basins by merger. Great Basins and Phillips agreed to terminate discussions on November 3, 1980, following the refusal by the Governor in Council of Canada to permit Phillips to acquire Great Basins' Canadian subsidiaries. Subsequent efforts to find a purchaser for Great Basins' shares or assets resulted in the proposal to purchase the Canadian Petroleum Subsidiaries. First Boston knows of no other, and has been informed by the management of Great Basins that there have been no other, proposals from any party more favorable than that set forth above.

In arriving at our opinion, we have reviewed certain publicly available business and financial information relating to Great Basins, including the Great Basins Proxy Statement. We have also reviewed certain other information supplied to us by Great Basins, including certain reports of independent consultants prepared for Great Basins and financial information prepared by Great Basins relating to the development or expansion of certain of its properties. We have met with the management of Great Basins to discuss the foregoing information with them. In connection with our review, we have not independently verified any of the foregoing information and have relied on its being complete and accurate in all material respects. With respect to the reports of independent consultants furnished to us by Great Basins, we have assumed, among other things, that they represent the best present estimates of Great Basins' hydrocarbon and other reserves addressed therein. In addition, we have not made an independent evaluation of the assets of Great Basins.

We have also considered, among other matters we deemed relevant, market data relating to trading in the Common Stock of Great Basins and the financial terms of certain other business combinations which have recently been effected.

Based on our analysis of the foregoing, it is our opinion that the proposed financial terms of the proposed sale of Great Basins' Canadian Petroleum Subsidiaries are fair from a financial point of view to the shareholders of Great Basins.

Very truly yours,

THE FIRST BOSTON CORPORATION

Lehman Brothers Kuhn Loeb
Incorporated

One William Street
New York, N.Y. 10004

March 10, 1978

The Board of Directors
Austral Oil Company Incorporated
2700 Exxon Building
Houston, Texas 77002

Gentlemen:

You have asked for our opinion with respect to the fairness to the stockholders of Austral Oil Company Incorporated ("Austral") of the proposed sale of properties of Austral to The Superior Oil Company ("Superior") and the related Plan of Complete Liquidation and Dissolution (the "Plan").

The terms and conditions of the proposed sale of properties pursuant to an Agreement for Sale of Properties between Austral and Superior as well as a description of the proposed plan of liquidation are set forth in a Proxy Statement prepared in connection with the Special Meeting of Stockholders of Austral which has been called to approve the Plan.

We have been in continuous discussion with Austral management through every step of the implementation of the Plan including negotiation with all of the potential purchasers. We have reviewed in depth the various opportunities available to Austral. Further, we are generally familiar with the terms of comparable transactions as well as the outlook for oil and gas producing companies both in the United States and in other countries. We have accepted the estimates of hydrocarbon reserves provided to us by Austral's management and independent reservoir engineers.

Accordingly, it is our opinion that the proposed sale of properties and the related Plan are fair and reasonable to the stockholders of Austral.

Very truly yours,

LEHMAN BROTHERS KUHN LOEB
INCORPORATED

By   JAMES W. GLANVILLE

DEAN WITTER & CO. Incorporated
800 Wilshire Boulevard, Los Angeles, Ca 90017   Telephone (213) 486-4111

August 2, 1976

Board of Directors
Edgington Oil Company
2400 East Artesia Boulevard
Long Beach, California 90805

Gentlemen:

At your request, we have reviewed the terms of the proposed purchase by an affiliate of Buckeye Pipe Line Company ("Buckeye") of certain assets constituting substantially all of the business of Edgington Oil Company ("Edgington") pursuant to the terms and conditions of the Assets Purchase Agreement dated June 15, 1976 (the "Agreement") and the Plan of Complete Liquidation and Dissolution of Edgington Oil Company (the "Plan"), in order to determine whether, in our opinion, the proposed transaction with Buckeye as described in the Agreement and the contemplated liquidation of Edgington as described in the Plan will be fair and equitable to the stockholders of Edgington.

You have informed us that you have been advised by counsel that the Buckeye transaction will not be taxable to Edgington, except for certain investment credit and depreciation recapture, and that the proceeds distributed to the stockholders, other than securities dealers holding such stock as inventory, will be taxed to them at capital gains rates.

In conjunction with rendering this opinion, we have conducted such an investigation of Edgington as we deemed necessary, including an examination and analysis of, among other things, Edgington's financial position, results of operations dividend policy, stock price performance, and reports and other documents filed by Edgington under the Securities Act of 1933 and the Securities Exchange Act of 1934. In addition, we have held discussions with Edgington's management concerning Edgington's future prospects and have reviewed industry conditions (including regulatory developments) and prospects, the performance of companies similar to Edgington, and the terms of the proposed sale of assets. In connection with rendering this opinion we have relied upon Edgington for certain information regarding Edgington and the proposed transactions without independent verification of such information.

Based upon the foregoing, and assuming consummation of the proposed Agreement with Buckeye and the consummation of the proposed Plan of liquidation, it is our opinion that the proposed transactions will be fair and equitable to Edgington's shareholders.

Very truly yours,

DEAN WITTER & CO. INCORPORATED

BLYTH EASTMAN PAINE WEBBER
INCORPORATED
1221 AVENUE OF THE AMERICAS
NEW YORK, NEW YORK 10020
———
212-730-8500

April 3, 1980

Board of Directors
OKC Corp.
4835 LBJ Freeway
Dallas, Texas 75234

Gentlemen:

OKC Corp. ("OKC") has called a Special Meeting of Stockholders to consider adoption of the proposed Plan of Liquidation and Dissolution (the "Plan") of OKC as described in the Proxy Statement (the "Proxy Statement"). You have requested our opinion from the standpoint of the stockholders of OKC as to whether adoption of the Plan would be in their best interests.

We are familiar with OKC's financial position and operating results, having acted as financial advisor to its Board of Directors and management on various occasions, including as an advisor during the negotiations leading to the agreement for sales of the OKC cement properties as described in the Proxy Statement. We have investigated OKC's divisions and subsidiaries and have discussed with management of OKC its future prospects and probable values of the refinery operation, its real estate holdings and its investments in oil and gas exploration activities. We have also reviewed conditions and prospects in the cement and oil refinery industries and the terms of the proposed Plan. In connection with rendering this opinion, we have relied upon OKC for certain information regarding OKC and the proposed liquidation without independent verification of such information.

We have also considered, among other matters we deemed relevant, the historical price ranges, dividend records and earnings per share of OKC's common stock and the effect of the announcement of the proposed Plan, its adoption by OKC's Board of Directors and the partial implementation of the Plan on the market price of OKC's common stock. We have considered alternative courses of action available to OKC and the possible impact of such alternatives.

Based upon the foregoing, it is our opinion that the proposed liquidation of OKC contemplated in the Proxy Statement and the Plan is in the best interests of the OKC stockholders.

Very truly yours,

BLYTH EASTMAN PAINE WEBBER
Incorporated

Index

ABOUT THE AUTHOR

RONALD J. KUDLA is a Professor of Business Administration in the Department of Business Administration at the University of Wisconsin–Eau Claire. He is one of the authors of *Corporate Spin-Offs: Strategy for the 1980s* (Greenwood Press, 1984) and *Cases in Financial Management*. His articles have appeared in the *Quarterly Review of Economics and Business, Journal of Business Finance and Accounting, The Academy of Management Journal*, and *Sloan Management Review*.